WHAT LEADERS SAY ABOUT *THE BIBLE COMPANION*

The Bible Companion's creative and relevant insights will shift your daily Scripture study from a "have to" to a "want to." *The Bible Companion*'s invitation to experience one chapter of Scripture per day helps you fall in love with God's unfolding story and empowers you for everyday faith.

—Kara Powell, chief of leadership formation at Fuller Theological Seminary
Executive director of the Fuller Youth Institute
Co-author of *3 Big Questions That Change Every Teenager*

The Bible Companion is well-named. Like a friend who loves the Bible from cover to cover, this series will stay by you as you read all sixty-six books as one story. The books will give you fresh insights on familiar passages as well as help you discern the stories embedded in those hard-to-read books, like Numbers and Ezekiel. If you want to see the Bible with fresh eyes, this is for you.

—Janice Cunningham Rogers, founder of Youth With A Mission School of Writing
Author of *Is That Really You, God?*

Karen Moderow's insights and the easy-to-follow format will help us to establish rhythms of Scripture engagement that will take us to depths we long to go but haven't had a path to take us there. *The Bible Companion* is a trusted friend that will accompany us on our journey to understanding the very heart of God through Scripture, revealing His love and purposes for us.

—Dr. Beverly Upton Williams, CEO of Haggai International

When the church is open to the Holy Spirit and God's Word, we will see the greatest awakening in history (Hab. 2:14). As pastors and leaders, we need *The Bible Companion* like never before to help eradicate biblical illiteracy. This series helps believers see the panorama of God's story with His special creation—us.

—Loren Cunningham, founder of Youth With A Mission (YWAM) International
Co-founder of the global University of the Nations

Christian people want and need the Bible to become their book. That is an exciting, if daunting, challenge. *The Bible Companion* offers just the accompaniment many readers need. It is a wonderful resource that walks with Bible readers as they make their way through either the whole or parts of the Bible. By all means, take up its offer, then walk in the light of God's Word.

—Mark Labberton, president of Fuller Theological Seminary

WHAT READERS SAY

Never have I been so captivated by the integration of big-picture patterns with the fine details of the Bible's stories as with *The Bible Companion*. Karen Moderow's approach is bold, realistic, and truth seeking. *The Bible Companion* is a fantastic resource for first-time readers or for those ready for a deeper-level study.

—Michael Pavlisin, founder of Impact Through Awareness

Growing up as a Christian, I'd read parts of the Bible, but reading the Bible all the way through seemed very intimidating. Daily readings in *The Bible Companion* help to break down the chapters one by one, in digestible bite-sized pieces. It highlights the main points, explains the key takeaways, and provides relatable guidance that I can apply to my own life. This series has made me excited to read more and learn more. It's reinvigorated my relationship with God and provided a great opportunity to share the experience with friends and loved ones. It's a beautiful feeling to grow closer to God again—thank you, *Bible Companion*!

—Armine Kourouyan, senior project manager for USC Hollywood, Health & Society

Karen Moderow's beautifully and intelligently crafted Bible series revolutionized my personal devotions. I've read the Bible through, but was looking for fresh insights and help understanding difficult books, like Leviticus. *The Bible Companion* walked me through parts of Scripture I had stumbled through before. The series helped me see a loving, invested God woven throughout Scripture from the first page to the last. *The Bible Companion* has given me a greater love for the Word of God. I wholeheartedly recommend it.

—Blossom Turner, Christian fiction author

BOOK 1
GENESIS—EXODUS

THE BIBLE COMPANION
Journey through Scripture One Day at a Time

God in Story
WHO WE ARE

BOOK 1
GENESIS–EXODUS

KAREN WESTBROOK MODEROW

Published by Redemption Press, PO Box 427, Enumclaw, WA 98022.
Toll-Free (844) 2REDEEM (273-3336)

Redemption Press is honored to present this title in partnership with the author. The views expressed or implied in this work are those of the author. Redemption Press provides our imprint seal representing design excellence, creative content, and high-quality production.

The author has tried to recreate events, locales, and conversations from memories of them. In order to maintain their anonymity, in some instances the names of individuals, some identifying characteristics, and some details may have been changed, such as physical properties, occupations, and places of residence.

Artwork by Kristine Brookshire.

ISBN 13: 978-1-64645-602-4 (Paperback)
978-1-64645-601-7 (ePub)
978-1-64645-600-0 (Mobi)

Library of Congress Catalog Card Number: 2021925804

DEDICATION

For my father, Pastor Floyd Westbrook,
who wrote the early versions of this series,
whose love for the Lord drew me to Christ, and
whose passion for God's Word inspired the faith of many.

BOOKS IN THIS SERIES

Set 1. God in Story: WHO WE ARE (Books of the Law)
  Book 1 Genesis, Exodus
  Book 2 Leviticus, Numbers, Deuteronomy

Set 2. God in History: LIVING FREE (Books of History)
  Book 3 Joshua, Judges, Ruth, Samuel
  Book 4 Kings, Chronicles, Ezra, Nehemiah, Esther

Set 3. God in Poetry: LIVING WISELY (Books of Wisdom)
  Book 5 Job
  Book 6 Psalms
  Book 7 Proverbs, Ecclesiastes, Song of Songs

Set 4. God in Warnings: CHOOSING LIFE (Books of the Prophets)
  Book 8 Isaiah, Jeremiah, Lamentations, Ezekiel
  Book 9 Daniel – Malachi

Set 5: God in Jesus: THE ULTIMATE REVELATION (The New Testament)
  Book 10 Matthew, Mark, Luke, John
  Book 11 Acts, Romans, Corinthians, Galatians, Ephesians, Philippians
  Book 12 Colossians—Revelation

TABLE OF CONTENTS

ACKNOWLEDGMENTS

I HAVE NOT WRITTEN THIS SERIES alone. A host of people have contributed to my faith, life experiences, and education in ways that are reflected in my writing.

I am most grateful for the love and legacy of my father, Pastor Floyd Westbrook. Without his teachings, example, inspiration, and prayers, this series would not exist.

I thank my husband, Joe, for his unwavering belief in me. He not only encourages my gifts but guards my time. His wisdom and practical support—filling in the gaps when life presses in—makes it possible for me to write.

My son, David, spent months transcribing my father's notes from Excel into Word so I could access them for this project. David's work, a labor of love, represents the passing of a spiritual legacy from one generation to another.

Since childhood, my brother, Ed Westbrook, has been my go-to person for help in a crisis. As I've worked my way through this series, he has rescued me numerous times from wrong approaches and missed deadlines. He is also responsible for many of the *Companion Thought* questions asked in these books.

Working with my niece, Kristine Brookshire, as she created the artwork for *The Bible Companion* has been a delight. She's brought the elements of style and beauty to the book covers I imagined. That she is family makes her contribution to this project especially dear to me.

Several people have been praying for me and this series for years—Lilian Reid, Vivian Henderson, Lauren-Jean Elsberry, Susan Hickey, Doreen Cox, and Cindy Westbrook. May God bless them for their faithful intercession.

A special thanks goes to fellow author Blossom Turner, who has carefully critiqued these books, reading them a chapter a day as they are meant to be read. Her knowledge of the Bible, editing skills, and thirst for God has made her the perfect "beta reader."

I am grateful for my friend, Elizabeth DeBeasi, whose honesty, love, intelligence, and professionalism continues to make me a better person and writer.

I am indebted to friends who gather in my home for *Bible and Breakfast*. We've experienced Christ as we've broken bread together and walked through Scripture using *The Bible Companion*. This beautiful group embodies the kind of community I pray this series will foster.

To my Redemption Press team, Cynthia Cavanaugh, Sara Cormany, Dori Harrell, Tisha Martin, Paul Miller, Carole Leathem, and Micah Juntunen—thank you for bringing my vision to life.

Sharon Brookshire, my sweet sister and faithful advocate, holds a special place in my heart. I start every morning knowing that she is praying for me. Her example of obedience, servanthood, and courage, despite brain cancer, humbles me. She inspires me to live what I write about.

My oldest son, Michael, and my brother-in-law, Ray, round out my tribe. Michael's daily gifts of coffee and tea keep me going. Ray brings refreshment of another sort. A consummate "gamer," Ray lures me away from my computer for much needed "fun breaks." These respites keep me sane.

Finally, I give thanks to God the Father, Son, and Holy Spirit for giving me the desire, strength, and resources to write *The Bible Companion*. The time we have enjoyed together is its own reward.

FROM THE AUTHOR

LET'S BE HONEST—THE BIBLE CAN be daunting. It's a big book. Some parts confuse us. Other parts (dare we say it?) can be boring. We also love to reread our favorite passages. But that verse from 2 Timothy nags at us—"*All* Scripture is given by inspiration of God, and is profitable for doctrine, for reproof, for correction, for instruction in righteousness" (2 Tim. 3:16 NKJV). We want to know what God says, but too often our good intentions fail when we reach Leviticus. If we're going to read the Bible all the way through, most of us need encouragement to make it through the hard parts. We also need accountability to establish the habit of Bible reading. *The Bible Companion* helps with both.

The Bible is a story. It starts with creation (Genesis) and ends with God rescuing men and women from a fight-to-the-death battle between good and evil (Revelation). How God ultimately redeems and transforms His creation opens our eyes to who God is. It also reveals who we are. A drama of love, betrayal, failure, and victory comes to life in the pages of Scripture.

There are many ways to read the Bible, but reading it from beginning to end connects us to God's bigger story. In Scripture, God reveals His plan for His creation through stories that build on one another. *The Bible Companion* keeps the story thread visible as you move from one book to another. The series' insights for each chapter pull you back into God's Word day after day.

As the Holy Spirit brings God's story to life, you'll find Bible reading a life-altering journey. There's no reading schedule. No checklist. If you miss a day, just pick up where you left off. The journey will be richer if you take a friend, your family, or a small group with you. The goal is doable. Small portions, every day.

Even if you've tried reading through the Bible before, try again. You're not alone this time. We can do it together.

Karen Westbrook Moderow

HOW TO USE THIS BOOK

THIS BOOK IS DESIGNED TO give you freedom to explore Scripture in ways that best suit you. The series is not a commentary or a devotional, though it has some elements of both—it's a companion. We will walk through the Bible together, asking the Holy Spirit to be our guide.

Read the Scripture first. Pay attention to how you react to the text—good, bad, or indifferent. Listen for any insights God gives you about what you read or what you feel. Then turn to *The Bible Companion.* You may want to use the book in one of these ways:

- Personal Journal: Record your spiritual journey.
- Legacy Journal: Make notes with future generations in mind.
- Family Journal: Read with the family, and have one or more of you write or draw something related to the chapter on each page. You can sign and date entries to create a family record.
- Creative Meditation: Doodle, use sticker art, or paint to creatively "own" each chapter.
- Bible Study: Underline and make notes of truths you want to study more deeply.
- Respite: Enjoy the white space. Let an uncluttered page remind you to breathe and take in what you've been reading.

THE BIBLE: WHAT KIND OF BOOK IS IT?

THE BIBLE HAS SIXTY-SIX BOOKS that tell God's story. Over centuries, more than forty authors inspired by the Holy Spirit wrote about God and His unfailing love for us using historical narrative, stories, poetry, letters, dreams, visions, and many other forms. Does the type of writing matter? We don't think about it, but anytime we pick up a book, we interpret what we read based on the kind of book it is.[1]

Take this example of the first line of a story: "The woman squeezed through the door and crept into the darkened room where the child slept." If we are reading a mystery, we may suspect some sort of crime is about to occur. If the book is a parenting guide, we may assume the woman is a mother taking care not to wake her child. However, if we are reading a book on child psychology, another interpretation becomes possible. We might view the scene from the perspective of the child, who, if awakened, might be frightened.[2]

In the Bible, genre—the kind of book or passage we are studying—gives us a lens through which to read. Genre facilitates the message, telling us *who* and *what* is important. For example, histories highlight people and events, whereas the law focuses on God's standards. Genre also sets expectations.[3] We shouldn't expect the laws on animal sacrifice to have the same devotional impact as a poetic book like Psalms. Nor should we expect Psalms to have the time and place details we find in historical books like 1 and 2 Kings.

Different kinds of writing in the Bible allow us to experience God's truth from a variety of perspectives. Some types will appeal to us more than others. What attracts us may not draw someone else. Scripture's many genres assure that each of us will hear God's message in a way that resonates. Personal preference doesn't exempt us from reading all of God's Word, but paying attention to the type of passage we are reading can help us find value in every text.

It's a mistake to think that the parts of the Bible we find difficult are less inspired, have less truth, or are less relevant. While much of the Bible contains clear instruction, God also inspired men to write Scripture in ways that make us wonder. God's Word often raises questions that require us to engage with Him and each other. This interaction is what makes the Bible exciting.

For help in exploring some of the creative ways God shares His truth, look for the short *How To* sections throughout the series. You'll find suggestions on how to read different genres such as the genealogies, the law, poetry, and end time (apocalyptic) dreams and visions.

The psalmist prays, "Open my eyes that I may see wonderful things in your law" (Ps. 119:18). If we ask, the Holy Spirit will unlock some truth in everything we read. "For the word of God is alive and active. Sharper than any double-edged sword, it penetrates even to dividing soul and spirit, joints and marrow; it judges the thoughts and attitudes of the heart" (Heb. 4:12).

THE OLD TESTAMENT

THE THIRTY-NINE BOOKS OF THE Old Testament make up nearly 75% of the Bible, yet many of us have never read it through.[4] The reasons are understandable. The authors who lived in ancient Near Eastern times told God's story using language and symbols that are unfamiliar to us.[5] Without context, we may miss not only nuances, but the message and perspective of a passage. What little we do know of the culture and religion of that day may offend us. The violence in the Old Testament can also bias us against it. We may have heard that the God of the Old Testament is a God of wrath, and the God of the New Testament is a God of love. If we haven't explored the first three-quarters of the Bible, we will not see that a loving God is woven throughout Scripture from beginning to end.

Another barrier to reading the Old Testament is the misconception that it is irrelevant. Since Jesus did away with the ceremonial laws, we may wonder why we should read them. The answer is that the principles behind the laws lay the foundation for knowing God. The Old Testament teaches us to expect God to intervene in the affairs of our world. What could be more relevant? The men and women who encounter God, though in another time, are our brothers and sisters. Their stories are our stories. The consequences of sin and the struggle to hold to faith while living in a violent and evil world are universal.

We first encounter sin in the Old Testament, but we also get our first glimpses of grace. If we start with creation and let God tell His story through those who loved and obeyed Him, we see that He has always been about relationship. Without the Old Testament, we can't fully appreciate how the life, death, and resurrection of Jesus makes knowing God possible.

When it was written, the Old Testament upended the ancient world's view of God. Today, the Old Testament still challenges the assumptions we make about Him. Its narratives do not allow us to dismiss Him with platitudes. Instead, we must grapple with hard, uncomfortable realities. God's story cannot be told in a few verses or chapters, but as we make our way through the Old Testament, His faithfulness overcomes all. These early Scriptures assure us that God loves us and can handle the complexities of our lives.

If we're still wondering if the Old Testament is important, perhaps this analogy will help. Suppose we and our siblings had been separated from our father at birth and then united with him as an adult. We could immediately start building a relationship, but it would be limited until we could answer certain questions: *What is our father like? Can he be trusted? What happened to separate us? Is what others have told us about him true? Are we like him? Do we want to be?* We would have to search the past to answer these questions. The Old Testament is our spiritual past. Its stories reveal God's character, giving us a basis for trusting Him. The Old Testament also points to our future. The prophets' words prove that Jesus is the one God sent to save us from our sins (Isa. 53, Matt. 1:21). The Old Testament shows us that God's love is unstoppable. The forgiven men and women whose stories of redemption fill its pages will give us hope.

The Old Testament divides into four sections:

- The Books of the Law (the Pentateuch, the Books of Moses, or the Torah)
- The Books of History

- The Books of Poetry (Wisdom literature)
- The Books of the Prophets

Like the New Testament, the Old Testament is "God-breathed" (2 Tim. 3:16). We can trust it. However, be prepared to be challenged. The narratives, history, poetry, and prophecies of the Old Testament refute our narrow understanding of God. Instead, we will discover a God whose love, generosity, mercy, justice, and power exceed anything we could imagine. The Old Testament may shake us to the core, but it also plants us firmly in the hope of Christ and His coming kingdom.

THE BOOKS OF THE LAW

THE PENTATEUCH

In Hebrew, the first five books of the Bible are called Torah, meaning "law" or "instruction." They are also known as the Books of Moses, the Law, or the Pentateuch.[6] Pentateuch comes from a Greek word that means five-volume work. Ancient scrolls were limited in the amount of content they could contain. Genesis, Exodus, Leviticus, Numbers, and Deuteronomy were one literary composition, but because of its length, the manuscript was divided into five scrolls.[7]

The Pentateuch is one continuous narrative that begins with creation and ends with God bringing His people into the Promised Land. All the laws found in between are part of this great story. Even in the Old Testament, the Lord's commands are not stand-alone regulations, but laws given in the context of His love for us and ours for Him. Jesus says the most important commandment is, "Love the Lord your God with all your heart and with all your soul and with all your mind and with all your strength" (Mark 12:30). Apart from a relationship with God, the Law kills. With God, the Law leads to life (2 Cor. 3:6).

Each book in the Pentateuch highlights one aspect of God's nature.

Genesis:	He is SOVEREIGN
Exodus:	He is ALL-POWERFUL
Leviticus:	He is HOLY
Numbers:	He is KIND but STERN
Deuteronomy:	He is FAITHFUL

THE BOOK OF GENESIS

GENESIS MEANS "THE ORIGIN OR coming into being of something."[8] In Genesis, the opening book of the Old Testament, we read of the beginning of the universe, the beginning of the human race, the beginning of sin, the beginning of God's redemptive plan for man, and the beginning of the nation of Israel. God gives the principles of the Sabbath, marriage, and work, early in His story.[9] Genesis is the first of five books of the Bible known as the Pentateuch, meaning "five-volume book." Jews and Christians accept Moses as the primary author and compiler of Genesis, Exodus, Leviticus, Numbers, and Deuteronomy.[10]

The book of Genesis anchors the whole of Scripture. Many themes and subjects are introduced in the first three chapters that appear again in the last three chapters of Revelation, the final book of the Bible.

Early on, Genesis gives us a definition of faith: "Abram believed the Lord, and he credited it to him as righteousness" (Gen. 15:6). In Hebrews 11, the giants of faith are listed, and more than half of them appear first in the book of Genesis—not just as heroes, but as flawed men and women who struggle as we do. Through their stories we see our first glimpse of a good, merciful, just, and holy God. We see God reaching for His children again and again—healing, sustaining, and rescuing.

In Genesis we not only witness God as the all-powerful Creator, but discover we are *the beloved* in the world's greatest love story.

Genesis 1
IN THE BEGINNING—GOD

In the beginning God created the heavens and the earth.
    Genesis 1:1

THE BIBLE'S OPENING STATEMENT TELLS us that the universe and everything in it exists as a result of God's purpose and creative energy. Psalm 19:1 (NKJV) says, "The heavens declare the glory of God; and the firmament shows his handiwork." Everything we see in the world around us bears evidence of an involved Creator.

In the creation story we read of light, water, abundance, and fruitfulness. These symbols of life are woven throughout the Old Testament and are repeated in the New Testament as Jesus proclaims Himself to be the light of the world, the living water, the bread of life, the vine, and the source of life.[11]

In Genesis we sense God's care, joy, and delight in His creation as He pronounces His work "good." This perspective of life as *good* is one that will be tested as the story unfolds. It is also tested in our lives. What we see in Genesis, we experience today. God's work in our world, as it was from the beginning of creation, is good.

COMPANION THOUGHT
What is difficult but good in your life?

Genesis 2

GOD GIVES LIFE

And the Lord God . . . breathed into his nostrils the breath of life.
    Genesis 2:7

GOD MADE US IN HIS image. Though housed in a body made from the dust of the ground, the very breath of God gives us life. He created us as spiritual beings with the capacity for relationship with Him, a characteristic that distinguishes us from the lower animals. It is the breath of God within us that causes us to yearn for relationship with Him and for the wholeness that He embodies—community, perfection, and immortality. Despite the evil around us, we know we are made for something better. When we long for a world where all is right, just, and good, we are longing for God and His kingdom.

Genesis 2 unveils God's perfect world where rest is a holy ritual of life (v. 2), we live in relationship with our Creator and each other (v. 18), and work is a partnership with God (v. 19). The first whisper of tension comes in verse 17 when God tells man not to eat of the Tree of the Knowledge of Good and Evil. God's gift—freedom to choose—sends fear down our spines. We know what will happen because we know ourselves.

The writer notes in Genesis that Adam and Eve are naked and do not feel ashamed (v. 25). That will soon change. Adam's rebellion puts man at war with himself, God, and others. But for this brief moment, we glimpse life as it could've been—as God intended it to be. Today, God's breath within gives us hope of recovering what we've lost. His breath sustains us every moment of life, reminding us that He is near. He has not given up on the beautiful world He has created, and He has not given up on us.

COMPANION THOUGHT

Is rest a priority in your life? When was the last time you went a full day without working?

ADAM AND EVE

ADAM AND EVE ARE UNIQUELY created by God's hand—Adam of dust, Eve from Adam's rib. They are the first to become *one flesh* through the mysterious union of marriage. Together they rule over the kingdom God gave them, and together they make a choice to disobey God. Their choice results in the fall of man, a condition where man's natural inclinations take him toward sin and away from what is right and good.

Adam and Eve's disobedience contains all the elements of temptation and sin that are now part of our human experience—guilt, blame, and consequences. Adam blames Eve. She blames the serpent. But in the punishment that follows, God makes it clear that each person is responsible for their choices.

With sin comes guilt and a loss of innocence. Adam and Eve become aware of their nakedness and prepare coverings of fig leaves for their bodies. The Creator's response to their efforts is significant—God makes garments of skin and covers them. In this early stage of man's history, we learn that sin is costly—the innocent die for the guilty. Though driven from the garden, Adam and Eve have a less intimate but ongoing relationship with God. They teach their children to worship God with sacrifices (Gen. 4:3–4). Seth, the son born after the death of Abel, knows of the Creator, and many of his descendants follow in God's ways.

Adam and Eve show us where the path of disobedience leads. They also show us that God does not allow failure to be the end of our stories. Adam and Eve become part of God's great plan to restore all of creation through Jesus, the Savior who will come from their bloodline.

Genesis 3

AN IMPORTANT PROMISE

He will crush your head.
    Genesis 3:15

THE IDEAL WORLD GOD CREATES shatters as Adam and Eve eat the fruit of the Tree of the Knowledge of Good and Evil. Through their act of disobedience, sin enters the world, and because of their sin, comes death. In an instant, Adam and Eve are separated from God—a spiritual death—and every living thing begins a spiral of decay that will lead to physical death. The *good* God has created must now coexist with evil.

Immediately after the fall, God puts into motion a plan to reclaim all that has been lost. God tells the serpent (Satan)[12] that the seed of the woman "will crush your head" (Gen. 3:15). This is the first promise of a Savior given in Scripture.[13] Even as God pronounces judgment, He refuses to let us go. Jesus Christ's death and resurrection will one day restore humanity and all of creation to its former glory. Today, Jesus's sacrifice makes it possible for every person to enjoy the intimate relationship Adam and Eve once had with God (Rev. 3:20).

God's first question to Adam after the fall is, "Where are you?" (Gen. 3:9). Our Creator asks that same question of us. The first step toward accepting the redemption God offers to us is acknowledging we are hiding just like Adam and Eve. Because of our sin, we are naked, filled with shame, afraid, and angry. We fear that if others see us as we are, they will reject us. But God says, "Never will I leave you; never will I forsake you" (Heb. 13:5). We have only to come to Him.

COMPANION THOUGHT
What is the most trouble you've gotten into? Did the situation make you avoid people? Why?

Genesis 4
A GOOD QUESTION

Am I my brother's keeper?
    Genesis 4:9

WHEN GOD QUESTIONS CAIN ABOUT his brother Abel, Cain responds with a question of his own: "Am I my brother's keeper?" (Gen. 4:9). The biblical answer to Cain's question is "Yes." As human beings, we are not responsible for our brother's whereabouts or his actions, but we are responsible for our attitudes and actions toward him. Just as Cain's actions banish him from God's presence, any hate or malice we carry in our hearts toward another also separates us from God.

For most of us, the sin we commit against our brothers and sisters is not murder, but is indifference. Not caring has great consequences for others and ourselves. Following Cain's offspring, we see that a family and a community that does not care for one another breeds violence.

Jesus's priority during His ministry years was to create a band of believers who loved God and each other. Jesus says, "A new command I give you: Love one another. As I have loved you, so you must love one another. By this everyone will know that you are my disciples, if you love one another" (John 13:34–35). Love is the sign of God's presence and the foundation of God's church and kingdom. If we hate, resent, or ignore others, we are literally aiding the enemy. "Anyone who claims to be in the light but hates a brother or sister is still in the darkness. Anyone who loves their brother and sister lives in the light, and there is nothing in them to make them stumble" (1 John 2:9–10).

COMPANION THOUGHT
Who were you jealous of as a child? Why? Did your parents play favorites? Does God?

ENOCH

THERE ARE TWO MEN NAMED Enoch in the early chapters of Genesis: Enoch, the eldest son of Cain (Gen. 4:17–18) and Enoch, the son of Jared who is the father of Methuselah (the oldest person on record in the Bible [Gen. 5:23]). The two Enochs draw attention to the two lines of Adam—the line of Cain and the line of Seth.

The line of Cain produces Lamech, the first polygamist recorded in Scripture. Lamech boasts about killing a young man who had wounded him. The murder, a gross overreaction, appears to be one of multiple acts of violence that Lamech justifies as revenge for God's judgment upon Cain and his descendants (Gen. 4:23–24).

The second Enoch is a man of the opposite character. His line is of Seth, the third son of Adam and Eve. Though Cain's murder of Abel fractures the newly founded human race, Seth and his family lead the way to spiritual renewal. Immediately after Seth's birth, the Bible notes, "At that time people began to call on the name of the Lord" (Gen. 4:26).

The Old Testament record of Seth's Enoch is brief, but powerful. His life does not conclude with the phrase "and then he died," like the others in his genealogy.[14] Rather, we are told, "Enoch walked faithfully with God; then he was no more, because God took him away" (Gen. 5:24). The New Testament explains what happened. "By faith Enoch was taken from this life, so that he did not experience death: 'He could not be found, because God had taken him away.' For before he was taken, he was commended as one who pleased God" (Heb. 11:5).

Enoch lived in a day when there was no Bible, no Abrahamic covenant, no law of Moses, no prophets, and no knowledge of Christ. Yet through the oral traditions of faith passed down through his family, he comes to know God. At the end of Enoch's allotted days on earth, God lifts him from this life and brings him directly into His presence.

Enoch is a shining light in this early period of human history. His life becomes important in our personal stories as well. Enoch's great-grandson, Noah, will rescue our ancestors from a worldwide disaster.

While we don't know why God exempted Enoch from death and not others who have also been faithful, Enoch has become a symbol of hope for believers. Whether we die or remain on earth until Jesus returns, those of us who have a relationship the Lord will be transported into God's presence for eternity (1 Thess. 4:13–17).

HOW TO READ THE GENEALOGIES

FIVE CHAPTERS INTO GENESIS, WE come to the first lengthy genealogy of the Bible. There are many genealogies scattered throughout the Old Testament, but only two in the New Testament (Matthew 1 and Luke 3). Filled with names we can't pronounce, let alone remember, these genealogies can be stumbling blocks to reading the Bible through. But these passages offer us a great gift. Early on, we are forced to ask—why is this here? This simple question is a key principle for reading all of Scripture.

The genealogies of the Bible have some unique characteristics. Only a few give multiple branches of the family. Most follow one person's heritage, and once that line is established, the author frequently skips generations. For this reason, it's not advisable to use these records to count the number of generations between events. The Scripture tells us when the number of generations is important and notes it (Matt 1:17).[15]

If the genealogies are not primarily to count generations, what role do they play? They place God's story in the real world. Other religions emerged from myths and legends; the stories of God's people are rooted in history. It is true that the Bible reveals truth using different genres like parables, proverbs, and dreams, but a genealogy helps us tell the difference. Whenever we find a genealogy, we know we're reading about real people in real time.

Genealogies serve other purposes as well. They confirm prophecies foretelling the lineage of Jesus. They record the fates of the faithful versus the unfaithful. Following ancestral lines, we see that blessings and curses fall according to how people respond to God. We're reminded that God, even as He works out His plan in the universe, sees us as individuals.

Unexpected gems lie deep in the genealogies. We find the prayer of Jabez tucked into 1 Chronicles 4. Rahab, the harlot who hides the Israelite spies, is named among the ancestors of Jesus in Matthew 1. So is the Gentile woman, Ruth. Simply by mentioning these men and women who existed on the margins of power, the genealogies make a powerful and revolutionary statement—God's kingdom is for all.

Still, appreciating the genealogies may not help us make our way through them. They can't and shouldn't be read as a narrative. Rather, think of them as a photo library. How do we look at photographs? We flip through them, lingering only if there's someone we recognize or something that catches our attention. Skimming through these passages is a legitimate way to read them. We should look for the little comments found in between names and underline anything that stops us. Significant people, places, and events often show up elsewhere.

Appreciating difficult parts of Scripture is like putting a puzzle together. A passage's purpose may not be immediately clear, but if we pay attention and remain alert while asking the Holy Spirit to open God's Word to us, the picture will begin to take shape. Maybe not that day. But in time.

The genealogies are about connections—God's connection to His people and our connection to each other, especially in the community of faith. As we consider the names before us, God will give us insight into the significance they hold.

Genesis 5
A MAN WHO WALKED WITH GOD

Enoch walked with God; then he was no more, because God took him away.
    Genesis 5:24

ENOCH'S STORY IS ONE OF those "asides" found in a genealogy. The Bible tells us that only two people have left this world without dying—Enoch and Elijah. Both were translated, that is, taken directly up into the eternal presence of God. This will be the experience of all who are alive at Christ's coming: "We will not all sleep; but we will all be changed—in a flash, in the twinkling of an eye" (1 Cor. 15:51–52).

The chapter opens with a parallel—God makes human beings in His likeness, and Adam creates a son in his (Adam's) likeness. The genealogy that follows makes a point—parents beget children who are like them. Whatever we are at our core, we pass on to our children genetically and spiritually. Enoch's awareness of God did not happen in a vacuum. He came from the line of Seth whose people knew and honored God. Generations of godly tradition led Enoch to a relationship with God few have experienced.

We should never underestimate the power of our faith to influence our children and the generations to come. "But from everlasting to everlasting the Lord's love is with those who fear him, and his righteousness with their children's children—with those who keep his covenant and remember to obey his precepts" (Psalm 103:17-18).

COMPANION THOUGHT
What traits of your parents do you see in yourself? How are your children like you?

Genesis 6

A RIGHTEOUS MAN

Noah was a righteous man, . . . and he walked faithfully with God.
  Genesis 6:9

THOUGH GENESIS 4–6 GIVES US the backstory to the flood, it's not clear who all the characters are who offend God. One theory is that the sons of men are fallen angels. Another is that they are the sons of Cain (with the sons of God being the sons of Seth).[16] Regardless, men and women descend into such gross wickedness that God pronounces judgment—a flood that will destroy humankind and cleanse the earth.

In the midst of this corrupt society, God finds a man who is righteous. This man, Noah, saves his family and the entire human race from annihilation. His story contains a pattern of *sin–judgment–token of grace* we find throughout the Old Testament:[17] After the fall, God offers grace in clothing Adam and Eve to cover their shame; Cain, after murdering his brother, is given a mark that spares his life; Noah's ark is a *token of grace* that allows for a remnant of humanity to be saved.

We all sin. We all deserve death, but God's grace literally saves us. This truth, found in the story of the flood, is the heart of the gospel. "But where sin increased, grace increased all the more, so that, just as sin reigned in death, so also grace might reign through righteousness to bring eternal life through Jesus Christ our Lord" (Rom. 5:20–21).

COMPANION THOUGHT

Have you ever been given a "break"? Have you given grace to someone who didn't deserve it?

Genesis 7

NOAH'S OBEDIENCE

Noah did all that the Lord commanded him.
    Genesis 7:5

THIS IS THE SECOND TIME we read about Noah's obedience to the Lord (see Gen. 6:22).
    Throughout his lifetime. Noah is at odds with his generation. No one except his immediate family shares his faith or his lifestyle. For 120 years he preaches while building the ark, and in all those years, he has not one convert.

Noah is mentioned several times in the New Testament as an example of faith and perseverance. His love for God is matched by his love for his family. Noah "in holy fear built an ark to save his family" (Heb. 11:7). Through his faith and obedience, Noah saves himself, his family, and the generations that come after him.

As believers we will experience isolation, mocking, and even persecution. Standing up against a culture that praises what we deplore and hates what we love can make us fearful and lonely, but our obedience pleases God and cuts a path for our loved ones to follow. Jesus says, "In this world you will have trouble. But take heart! I have overcome the world" (John 16:33).

COMPANION THOUGHT
Is there something you feel God is calling you to do? What keeps you from doing it?

NOAH

As the human population of the earth increased, so did wickedness. "The earth was corrupt in God's sight and was full of violence" (Gen. 6:11). "The Lord saw how great the wickedness of the human race had become on the earth, and that every inclination of the thoughts of the human heart was only evil all the time" (Gen. 6:5).

As the people of Noah's day move further and further away from God, a spark of faith survives in Noah. He follows God's ways, living a godly life in contrast to the culture surrounding him. Scripture says, "Noah found favor in the eyes of the Lord. . . . [He] was a righteous man, blameless among the people of his time, and he walked faithfully with God" (Gen. 6:8–9). We are told, "Noah did everything just as God had commanded him" (Gen. 6:22).

Noah is the first person of record to receive a covenant from God. (Abraham and David will later be given covenants also.) The Noahic Covenant—God's unconditional promise to never again destroy all life on earth by flood—was made with Noah, his descendants, and all of God's creation. God gives the rainbow as a visible sign and perpetual reminder of that promise.

Noah is revered as one of the great men of the Bible. The record of his life spans five chapters in Genesis. In the New Testament, he is praised for his faith and obedience (Heb. 11:7; 1 Peter 3:20).

Genesis 8

AS LONG AS THE EARTH ENDURES

Seed time and harvest, cold and heat, summer and winter, day and night will never cease.
   Genesis 8:22

THE STORMS UNLEASHING TORRENTS OF water on the earth must have panicked men and women inside and outside the ark. Until this time, it had never rained on the earth. Genesis 2:6 says that the earth's vegetation had been watered by the dew of underground springs.

After the flood, Noah must have been apprehensive about what lay ahead. God, understanding his insecurities, gives Noah assurances about the future. First, God promises, "Never again will I destroy all living creatures, as I have done" (Gen. 8:21). Then He reestablishes the cycles of nature and promises they will exist as long as the earth stands.

Here, early in Genesis, we see two aspects of God that will anchor all of Scripture—His righteousness (which demands judgment for sin) and love. The account of the flood stands as both warning and encouragement. Genesis 8 begins, "God remembered Noah . . . ." God does not forget us when we are overwhelmed by life's storms. Sin may cause cataclysmic devastation, but God will act to rescue those who respond to Him in faith and obedience.

COMPANION THOUGHT
Would you describe yourself as being inside or outside the ark? Do you feel as if God has forgotten you?

Genesis 9

GOD'S RAINBOW

I have set my rainbow in the clouds.
    Genesis 9:13

GOD DOES NOT LEAVE NOAH to wonder what future he might have now that the world has been devastated by the flood. The Lord searches him out and blesses him (Gen. 9:1). (Blessing will be a theme throughout Genesis.)[18] What's more, God promises that He will never again destroy the earth by water. God's commitment is the first *covenant* found in Scripture. A covenant is a legal binding agreement between two parties.[19] God will use covenants at critical times in His story to reveal Himself and to teach us how to be in relationship with Him.[20] The covenant with Noah has its origins in the garden of Eden, where God made human beings the "rulers" of His world. Using the same language found in Genesis 1:26–28, God formally extends the authority He gave to Adam and Eve to those who have survived the flood (Gen. 9:1).

The honor and responsibility of caring for God's creation remains ours today. As God's children made in His image (Gen. 9:6), we are obligated to care for each other and for creation in a way that all will thrive. But whether we fulfill our end of the bargain or not, God promises that the cycles of nature will never cease and that He will never again destroy the earth by water. As a sign, God gives the rainbow (v. 13).

The flood gives a new start, but does not solve the world's problems. For the first time, drunkenness is mentioned (v. 21). An alcohol-related incident shames the "new Adam"[21] and brings a curse on his youngest son (v. 25). Symbolically, we humans survive, but so do our sinful natures. However, sin does not deter our Creator. His covenant with Noah tells us that sin has not altered God's plan for humanity. Though our capacity for evil is great, the rainbow witnesses that God's capacity for grace and redemption is greater.

COMPANION THOUGHT
What was the first agreement or contract you signed? Did you keep it?

God's Covenant with Noah

I establish my covenant with you:
Never again will all life be destroyed by the waters of a flood;
never again will there be a flood to destroy the earth.

Genesis 9:11

Genesis 10

THE HUMAN RACE IS ONE

These are the clans of Noah's sons. . . . From these the nations spread out over the earth after the flood.
    Genesis 10:32

THE GENEALOGIES AFTER THE FLOOD show God honoring His commitment to sustain His creation. Life goes on. People settle in diverse areas from the coast to mountains of Assyria and begin to develop their own languages and culture. Verse 9 tells us that God's story is being relayed from one generation to another. One man, Nimrod, is known as "a mighty hunter before the Lord" (Gen. 10:9). His name reflects his clan's reverence for God. They recognized the Creator as the one who provides and watches over them.

Through Noah, Adam's line flourishes. The apostle Paul says, "From one man [God] made all the nations, that they should inhabit the whole earth" (Acts 17:26). At our core, our needs and problems are the same regardless of our culture, ethnicity, gender, language, sophistication, or economic status. This commonality, our humanness, is the cornerstone for God's relational law: "Love your neighbor as yourself" (Mark 12:31). As we work through the Old Testament, we will see God's codes of behavior give dignity to every person. Human beings are to be respected simply because we are created in God's image.

Our humanity connects us to every human being who has ever lived or ever will live. When we hurt another, we hurt ourselves. "For none of us lives for ourselves alone, and none of us dies for ourselves alone" (Rom. 14:7).

COMPANION THOUGHT

How does humiliating someone deny them the dignity God gave them? Describe a time you have either been disrespected or have disrespected someone else. How do you feel about that experience now?

Genesis 11

DISPLACING GOD

Let us build ourselves a city, with a tower that reaches to the heavens, so that we may make a name for ourselves.

Genesis 11:4

NOAH'S DESCENDANTS DETERMINE TO BUILD a tower that reaches into the heavens. They believe they can penetrate God's realm and make a name for themselves that will put them above God. Pride drives them—the same sin that had motivated Lucifer to rebel against God (Luke 10:18; Isa. 14:12–14) and tempted Eve to "be like God" (Gen. 3:5). But the arrogance of the men and women of Babel is both shocking and laughable. Genesis 11:5 says, "The Lord came down." Nothing built by humans can ever reach God's abode. God doesn't interrupt the communication of the builders of the tower of Babel because He is threatened; He stops the builders to keep them from destroying themselves. The Message Bible says, "No telling what they'll come up with next—they'll stop at nothing!" (v. 6). We aren't told what their plans are, but God sees that the people of Babel are on a futile path.

Sometimes we don't understand why God thwarts our way. Even if we're not in open rebellion, we may pursue a course of action to our detriment. Pride tells us we know what's best, but trusting God means accepting His discipline even if it means abandoning our ideas. The interruptions that frustrate us may also redirect us. "'For I know the plans I have for you,' declares the Lord, 'plans to prosper you and not to harm you, plans to give you hope and a future'" (Jer. 29:11).

COMPANION THOUGHT

Have you ever tried to "make a name" for yourself, for a cause, or for a ministry in a bad way? What happened?

ABRAHAM

WHEN WE FIRST READ OF this patriarch in Genesis 11:26, his name is Abram. But God changes his name to Abraham, meaning "father of many," and promises to make of him a great nation (Gen. 17:5). Abraham is of the "godly" line of Seth (the son born to Adam and Eve after Abel was murdered).

Abram was born in Ur, modern day Iraq.[22] We're not told why, but at some point, Abram's father uproots the family from Ur, intending to go to Canaan. Mid-journey, they stop and settle in Harran, where Abram's father dies. Joshua 24:2 tells us the family worshiped idols.[23] Yet some knowledge of the One True God must have survived. When God tells Abram to leave his home and relatives and go to a land God will show him, Abram obeys. He takes his nephew, wife, servants, and all their possessions with him (Gen. 12:4). He enters Canaan not a poor nomad, but a wealthy tribal chief.[24]

After years in Canaan, God's promise still eludes him. Abraham has no heir. He owns no land. Yet we are told "[Abraham] staggered not at the promise of God through unbelief; but was strong in faith" (Rom. 4:20 KJV).

One of the greatest testaments to the patriarch's faith is that Abraham communicates God's promise to his descendants. The *promise*—given by a living, good, powerful, and relational God—becomes the cornerstone of the family's religion and culture.[25] This promise becomes the driving force behind the Jewish nation.

Genesis gives us the privilege of journeying with Abraham as he learns who God is and discovers that a personal relationship with Him is possible. Abraham comes to know God as "the Lord, before whom I have walked" (Gen. 24:40). In both the Old Testament and the New Testament, Abraham is called the friend of God (2 Chron. 20:7; James 2:23). In the give-and-take, the disappointment, and the sorrows that Abraham experiences, we learn of God's justice, righteousness, faithfulness, wisdom, goodness, and mercy.[26]

In the New Testament, Abraham is recognized as the father of all who believe (Rom. 4:16). He stands as a giant of faith whose vision extends beyond the land grant of Canaan. The patriarch's belief that God had something more, something better than what he could imagine, carries him when he doesn't understand. His faith secures him in values that are permanent and enduring. Abraham's compelling desire was that he and his posterity would participate positively in God's future. "For he was looking forward to the city with foundations, whose architect and builder is God" (Heb. 11:10).

Genesis 12
THE CALL OF ABRAHAM

All peoples on earth will be blessed through you.
    Genesis 12:3

THE CALL OF ABRAHAM, ONE of the most significant events in the Old Testament, marks the beginning of what will become the Hebrew nation. Around 2000 BC, Abram (later Abraham) is born in Ur. Ancient Ur was in the region of Mesopotamia, near the Euphrates River, just north of the Persian Gulf.[27] God calls Abram to leave his homeland. If he obeys, God vows to make him a great nation and promises that "all peoples on earth will be blessed through you" (Gen. 12:3). This is the second covenant God makes with a human being. The first covenant, given to Noah, affects all creation.[28] The covenant with Abraham is for the patriarch specifically, but will affect all people. With each covenant, we are learning more about God. He is not just a God who controls the cycles of nature, but He is a God who seeks a personal relationship with us.

Abram obeys, but imperfectly. In the infancy of faith, he makes mistakes. He leaves the land God has called him to when famine hits. In Egypt, he endangers his wife and himself with a lie. Yet God continues to teach him and assure Abraham that he will have children and inherit the land of Canaan. In time, Abraham will become the father of the Israelites, the Jews. His descendant, Jesus Christ, will come to earth as *the* blessing, *the* ultimate fulfillment of the Abrahamic promise (Gal. 3:16).

Like Abraham, we are blessed to be a blessing. God's gifts and resources are not just for our benefit—they are given to us in trust. Shared blessings of God's are expressions of Christ's love, signs of hope, and abundant mercy that point others to the Savior.

COMPANION THOUGHT
Are only ministers and pastors "called" by God? What is your calling?

God's Covenant with Abraham

I will make you into a great nation,
and I will bless you;
I will make your name great,
and you will be a blessing.
I will bless those who bless you,
and whoever curses you I will curse;
and all peoples on earth
will be blessed through you.

Genesis 12:2–3

Genesis 13

A PAINFUL PARTING

Let's not have any quarreling between you and me, . . . for we are close relatives.
Genesis 13:8

ABRAM HAS JUST RETURNED TO Bethel after a disastrous stay in Egypt (Gen. 12:10–20). Back in the land God has promised him, Abram offers sacrifices and seeks God's guidance (Gen. 13:4). Then a quarrel threatens the family. Though God had told Abram to leave his kindred behind, he'd brought his nephew with him. The Bible doesn't comment further about it, so it is unclear if God approved or not. Life soon separates them anyway. Strife between Lot and Abram's workers becomes intolerable, and Abram suggests an amicable parting (Gen. 13:9).

As the patriarch, Abram has the right to impose his will on his nephew, but doesn't. He allows Lot to take the choice land. Abram seems to be left with the dregs. Though Lot has prospered under his uncle's protection, he expresses no gratitude or any desire to reconcile. We can surmise that the crisis shook Abram because after Lot leaves, God appears and offers reassurance (vv. 14–17). God then tells Abram to walk the land. The act becomes a holy ritual. In walking the land, Abram acknowledges that his inheritance cannot be diminished by another's choices. Abram's hope is not in the land, but in God, who has promised it to him.

It is in times of deep disappointment that God comes to us, affirming His promises. He may ask us to do something that requires a step of faith. Trusting God brings blessing and fruitfulness, no matter how barren our lives may seem. God says, "I will make rivers flow on barren heights, and springs within the valleys. I will turn the desert into pools of water, and the parched ground into springs" (Isa. 41:18).

COMPANION THOUGHT
Do you have any family quarrels that need to end? What gesture on your part might help?

Genesis 14

THE MYSTERY PRIEST KING

Melchizedek . . . blessed Abram.
        Genesis 14:18–19

LOT, WHO NOW LIVES IN Sodom, is captured in a raid. Without hesitation, Abraham marshals his warriors and rescues Lot, his neighbors, and their belongings. As Abraham and his troops start home, they meet a man whose origins are unknown. This is unusual as family connections defined people of this era. We're told only that the mysterious Melchizedek is priest/king of Salem ("Salem" is a shortened form of Jerusalem).[29] In ancient times, kingly and priestly duties were often performed by the same person.[30] This Canaanite king evidently knows the One True God.

In Hebrews 5–7, Melchizedek is presented as a type of Christ. Melchizedek brings bread and wine (Gen. 14:18), symbols Jesus will later embody (1 Cor. 11:23–25). After the priest blesses Abram, the patriarch gives Melchizedek 10 percent of his bounty (the tithe). By paying tithes, Abram acknowledges that all he has comes from God's hand. Soon after, Abram is offered a reward from a pagan king. He refuses it. His choice to accept only what God gives him sends a message. God is his provider and his protector. He needs nothing from his pagan neighbors.

The principle of tithing, first given here, holds for us today. Returning a generous portion of what God has given us acknowledges God as the source of all. It also requires that we rely on Him to meet our needs. We invest in what we believe in. The choices we make with our money reveal who and what we trust. Jesus says, "No one can serve two masters. Either you will hate the one and love the other, or you will be devoted to the one and despise the other. You cannot serve both God and money" (Matt. 6:24).

COMPANION THOUGHT
How does your family react when a family member gets in trouble? How does your spending reflect your priorities?

Abram believed the Lord, and he credited it to him as righteousness.
Genesis 15:6

Genesis 15

ABRAM BELIEVES GOD

Abram believed the Lord, and he credited it to him as righteousness.
Genesis 15:6

AFTER RESCUING LOT AND FIVE neighboring kings, Abram returns home with trepidation. He is a vulnerable nomad. The possibility of ongoing battles with those he defeated must worry him. "Do not be afraid," God says. "I am your shield, your very great reward" (Gen. 15:1). The mention of reward triggers Abram's frustration. His response suggests he's fighting bitterness and disillusionment. The reward God has promised him is children, and he has none.

God assures him "a son who is your own flesh and blood will be your heir" (Gen. 15:4). He promises that Abram's descendants will be countless, like the stars. Though by now it's obvious Abram and Sarai cannot have children, Abram believes God.

The sacrifice described at the end of this chapter seems strange to us, but Abram would've recognized the ritual as a Near Eastern blood covenant, the Covenant of Pieces. The ritual seals the terms of a contract. By walking between the slaughtered animals, the two parties are saying, "May the same happen to me if I fail to keep these promises."[31] Yet here, only God—seen as a smoking fire pot and a flaming torch—passes through the dead animals. He seals both sides of the covenant. No other party has obligations.

The Abrahamic Covenant foreshadows the work of the cross, where Jesus alone fulfills all the promises of the Old Testament covenant. The promises of family, inheritance, and blessing that were first given to Abram now spiritually extend to all who believe. God alone seals the covenant. "For it is by grace you have been saved, through faith—and this is not from yourselves, it is the gift of God—not by works, so that no one can boast" (Eph. 2:8–9).

COMPANION THOUGHT
If you could "shake hands" with God to seal a deal, what deal would it be?

Genesis 16

A DIFFICULT SITUATION

Go back to your mistress.
    Genesis 16:9

AT SARAI'S INSISTENCE, ABRAM TAKES Hagar as his wife. When the slave girl becomes pregnant, she challenges Sarai and loses. We cringe as Abram stands by and allows Sarai to abuse the girl. Desperate, Hagar flees. But God—described as the Angel of the Lord—comes looking for her. He tells the slave girl to go back to her mistress and to submit to her. Unprotected in the desert, Hagar could not survive.

Though Hagar returns to the household where she is hated, things are not the same. God has seen her. He knows her name. He has made promises to her. No matter what Sarai may do to her, Hagar now has hope—the son she carries will also be a great nation.

If there's one thing Hagar's story tells us, it's that there's no one-size-fits-all approach to difficult circumstances. There are times we must leave abusive situations, but we can also be too quick to remove ourselves from difficult people when a more mature course might be to stay and work through the problem. Such choices are not easy, and we must be mindful that fewer options exist for those who are less powerful. For ourselves, whether we go or stay, an encounter with God makes the difference. God sees our plight and knows our name. He reminds us that the blessings He's promised belong to us and to our children. No one can take them from us.

COMPANION THOUGHT
What is the most difficult choice you've ever made? Why?

Genesis 17
GOD'S COVENANT WITH ABRAHAM

I will establish my covenant . . . between me and you and your descendants.
    Genesis 17:7

ABRAM IS NOW NINETY-NINE, AND any hope of having a child is gone. When God appears to him and repeats the promise, Abram falls on his face. He's past words. Past understanding. But God carries on. He not only affirms the covenant, but wants Abram to be circumcised as a sign that he believes. As if Abram and Sarai's barrenness isn't humiliation enough, the new names God gives them highlights their ironic status. Abram, the childless patriarch, becomes Abraham, *father of many*. Sarai (meaning "contentious") becomes Sarah (meaning "princess"). *Princess* assumes a kingdom.[32] Impossible. But God clarifies her role. Sarah will be the mother of the promised son. At this word, Abraham falls on the ground laughing. Then gathering himself, he offers Ishmael as the son of promise, but God says no. "This time next year, Sarah your wife will have a son" (Gen. 18:10). Despite initial skepticism, Abraham believes God. As an act of faith, Abraham is circumcised along with the males of his household.

The covenant terms of Genesis 17 become the charter of the Jewish nation.

The covenant:

1. is based on God's revelation of Himself as God Almighty (v. 1);
2. promises to make Abraham's family great (v. 2);
3. is everlasting (v. 7);
4. includes Abraham's descendants (v. 7);
5. is tied to the land of Israel (v. 8); and
6. is sealed with the sign of circumcision (v. 10).

In the New Testament, circumcision is defined as spiritual, a condition of the heart (Rom. 2:28–29). To be circumcised in the heart means we are willing to cut away anything that does encourage our relationship with God.

COMPANION THOUGHT
Are you skeptical about God's promises? Has God asked you to do something hard as a sign that you believe He will come through for you? What?

Genesis 18

TRUSTING THE JUSTICE OF GOD

Will not the Judge of all the earth do right?
    Genesis 18:25

GENESIS 18 REPORTS TWO EVENTS. The first—announcing that within a year Sarah will have a son—reveals God as a miracle worker. "Is anything too hard for the Lord?" (Gen. 18:14). The second—announcing the destruction of the wicked—reveals God as a trustworthy judge. "Will not the Judge of all the earth do right?" (v. 25).

Abraham and Lot live opposite lives. To Abraham, God is a miracle worker, but to Lot, God is a judge. God notes that Abraham can be trusted to teach his children to follow God's commands (v. 19). Lot, however, has allowed his family to be absorbed into Sodom's pagan culture (Gen. 19). Sodom and Gomorrah are so wicked that God determines to destroy both cities. When God tells Abraham, Abraham pleads with God to spare Sodom for the sake of fifty people. God agrees to fifty. Then forty-five. Then forty. Abraham bargains down to ten. God knows there are not ten righteous people in Sodom, but He is making a point. By inviting Abraham into the judgment process, God allows Abraham (and us) to see that He is not capricious.

The Bible tells us that there will be a day when all men will stand before God and be judged: "Each of us will give an account of ourselves to God" (Rom. 14:12). Judgment seldom falls as we think it should, but Genesis 18 teaches us that God is compassionate. He does not jump to judgment. He delays. He listens. He gives opportunity for repentance. There is a day of judgment, but when it comes, we can be assured that the Judge of all the earth is doing what is right.

COMPANION THOUGHT
What would you have done if the decision to judge Sodom and Gomorrah was yours? Why?

Is anything too hard for the Lord?
Genesis 18:14

Genesis 19

THE MAN WHO LOSES EVERYTHING

Lot . . . spoke to his sons-in-law, . . . but his sons-in-law thought he was joking.
  Genesis 19:14

WHEN THE ANGELS INFORM LOT that Sodom will be destroyed, he tries to warn his family. But his family scoffs. Lot has lost whatever influence he once had with them.

One unwise choice started Lot on the path that led to this day. He knew of Abraham's call and the importance of following God's ways. As a young man, he'd forsaken the security of a homeland for the future God had promised and prospered. But when he separated from Abraham, Lot stepped away from God. The Bible says, he "pitched his tents near Sodom" (Gen. 13:12). Even then, Sodom was known for its wickedness. He soon moved into the city (Gen. 14:12) Over time, Lot became comfortable with the perverted and sinful lifestyles of Sodom, even joining Sodom's ruling council.[33]

When Sodom is destroyed, Lot barely escapes with his life. But tragically, he loses everything else—his wife, the respect of his family, his home, and his wealth. Finally, he loses all decency, and in a drunken stupor, commits incest with his daughters.

God tells Abraham, "I am your shield" (Gen. 15:1). The shield is an image often repeated in the Psalms (Ps. 3:3; 33:20; 84:11; 115:9). God does not force us to stay under His protection. He allows us to make choices. If we opt to identify with the world, we put ourselves and our loved ones at risk. But if we choose the Lord, God marshals the armies of Heaven to protect us and all we have committed to Him.

COMPANION THOUGHT

Have you ever been tempted to "pitch your tent near Sodom"? What did you do? How did it compromise you or your family?

Genesis 20

ABRAHAM, THE FIRST PROPHET

He is a prophet, and he will pray for you.
        Genesis 20:7

GOD WARNS ABIMELECH IN A dream that Sarah is Abraham's wife. In ancient cultures, taking another man's wife meant death. God tells the shaken king, "Abraham is a prophet, and he will pray for you." This is the first mention of the title *prophet* in Scripture.[34] In both the Old and the New Testaments, prophets are spiritual leaders to be respected and obeyed. It's significant that God refers to Abraham as a prophet, even though the patriarch is in the midst of a major failure.

Because of Abraham's actions, Sarah has suffered the humiliation and uncertainty of harem life. Abimelech has been compromised. When the king asks for an explanation, Abraham says, "When God called me to leave my father's home and to travel from place to place, I told [Sarah], 'Do me a favor. Wherever we go, tell the people that I am your brother'" (Gen. 20:13 NLT). Abraham hasn't just lied once or twice, but has lied many times. His cowardly behavior reveals a pattern of protecting himself rather than trusting God. Now everyone knows. Even though Abimelech is innocent, the king, fearing God will hold him accountable, scrambles to make things right (vv. 14–16). Abraham does pray for him, and the prophet's prayer releases the curse of barrenness that Sarah's presence in Abimelech's house had caused.

God protects us when we stumble, but He will also expose our sin. Our failures do not disqualify us from God's calling; they humble us. They give us opportunities to deal with sin and commit to integrity. They foster honesty between us and others. They teach us that God heals. Whether we are the innocent or guilty one, if we've been derailed by the consequences of sin, God can put us back on the path of blessing.

COMPANION THOUGHT

What mistake have you made more than once? Have someone's prayers helped you get back on track? Who do you pray for and why?

Genesis 21

GOD OPENED HER EYES

Then God opened her eyes and she saw a well of water.
Genesis 21:19

THE SLAVE GIRL, HAGAR, WHO finds herself a pawn in her masters' plans, is one of the saddest stories in the Bible. Ishmael's birth gives her some security—or so she thinks. For thirteen years, her son has been the child of promise and the apple of Abraham's eye. But suddenly, she and her son are cast out. Stranded in the desert without water and near death, the lad cries out. God hears him. God speaks to Hagar, assuring her that they will survive and that her son Ishmael will become a great nation. Then God opens her eyes, and she sees a well. Blinded by her tears and overwhelmed by her problems, Hagar hadn't seen the water, which had been there all the time.

We sometimes pray for a miracle when what we really need is the ability to see and utilize the resources around us. The provision of God comes from many places and exceeds what we ask for. God gives us more than temporary solutions—He offers an abundant supply! "This is the confidence we have in approaching God: that if we ask anything according to his will, he hears us. And if we know that he hears us—whatever we ask—we know that we have what we asked of him" (1 John 5:14-15).

COMPANION THOUGHT
What problems are you facing that seem to have no solution? Have you asked God to "open your eyes"?

ISAAC

ISAAC, THE HEIR GOD PROMISED Abraham, is the least prominent of all the patriarchs, but is a vital link in the chain. He receives not only material wealth from his father, but also the spiritual riches of faith. In turn, Isaac teaches his family to know and worship the One True God.

Isaac was probably in his early teens when he traveled with his father to Mount Moriah. He knows the purpose of the journey is to make a sacrifice, and he asks his father why they have brought no animal. Abraham then makes one of the most profound prophetic statements of Christ's coming in Scripture: "God himself will provide the lamb for the burnt offering, my son" (Gen. 22:8). However, in that moment, Abraham believes his beloved son, Isaac, will be offered. We don't know at what point Isaac realized he was to be the sacrifice, but he must have agreed to the plan. Certainly the boy was old enough to overpower the aged Abraham. Isaac trusts his father and trusts God, who indeed spares his life.

In Scripture, Isaac is eclipsed by his powerful father, Abraham, and his colorful son, Jacob. Prior to his marriage, Isaac's life is a part of Abraham's narrative. After his marriage, Isaac's life becomes part of the story of Jacob.

Theologically, Isaac is an important figure. In Galatians 4:21–31, Paul uses Isaac to represent Christians who are justified by faith. Trying to obtain righteousness through the law makes us like Ishmael, who is born of the bondwoman, Hagar. Freeborn heirs, represented by Isaac, receive their spiritual inheritance through the promise, not the law.

From a spiritual standpoint, we identify with Isaac. We have no merit of our own, but because of our relationship with our Father, we inherit everything.

Genesis 22

GOD WILL PROVIDE

God himself will provide the lamb.
      Genesis 22:8

AFTER WAITING FOR SO LONG for his son, Abraham now believes God is requiring him to give up Isaac. But Abraham tells his servants, "We will worship and then we will come back to you" (Gen. 22:5). He must have trusted that God would either raise Isaac from the dead or make another way. When Isaac questions his father about the sacrifice, Abraham answers prophetically: "God himself will provide the lamb for the burnt offering" (v. 8).

God provides a ram for Abraham's offering (v. 13), but the ram foreshadows the ultimate sacrifice God will provide. God will send His own Son, Jesus, as a sacrificial lamb to be slain for the sins of the world (John 1:29). Abraham's test had greater implications than Abraham could have imagined. Our tests, too, may impact others in ways we don't see. They certainly reveal if anything stands between us and God.

God knows our hearts, but it is hard for us to discern our motives. Jeremiah 17:9 says, "The heart is deceitful above all things. . . . Who can understand it?" Testing is not so much for God's benefit as ours. How we respond under pressure clarifies what we most love and where our loyalties lie. Testing proves who we are to ourselves and gives God the opportunity to prove Himself to us.

We may wonder how God can accomplish what He's promised when what we most value in life is being destroyed. The Bible teaches that in a moment, God can resurrect what was dead. He can make a way where no path is visible. He can meet our physical, spiritual, and emotional needs. We can trust Him. "He who did not spare his own Son, but gave him up for us all—how will he not also, along with him, graciously give us all things?" (Rom. 8:32).

COMPANION THOUGHT
Can you think of a time when something you thought disastrous worked out in your favor?

Genesis 23

A BURIAL PLACE FOR SARAH

I will pay the price of the field . . . so I can bury my dead there.
Genesis 23:13

ABRAHAM IS THE RECIPIENT OF one of the largest land grants in history. God had said to him, "The whole land of Canaan, where you now reside as a foreigner, I will give as an everlasting possession to you and your descendants after you" (Gen. 17:8).

Yet when Abraham's wife dies, he owns not a single plot of land. His Hittite neighbors offer to give him a tomb, but Abraham refuses. Perhaps he's thinking about the future. When he is gone, how will his descendants know of their connection to the land? A gift gives him no rights. Buying a prominent burial site does. The owner drives a hard bargain. He won't sell unless Abraham buys not only the cave, but also the surrounding lands—and the price is exorbitant. Still, Abraham agrees to the terms, not haggling as was the custom. The cave at Machpelah gives Abraham a foothold in the Promised Land. Generations of Abraham's descendants will be buried there, including his great-grandson, Joseph. Sarah's death pressed Abraham toward God's intended goal. The purchase of the burial site establishes Canaan as the Jews' ancestral home.

Tragedies put us in situations we wouldn't choose, but they also create unexpected opportunities. Sorrow and loneliness may lead us to people and places we would otherwise miss. Difficult circumstances force us to grow, to put down roots in a new environment. Our comfort is in knowing that God has a future for us. We may still feel as though we don't belong and as if things aren't as they should be, but one day we will inherit all that God has promised.

COMPANION THOUGHT

Does your family have an ancestral burial place? Do you think death rituals are important in helping us deal with the loss of loved ones? Why or why not?

Genesis 24
A BEAUTIFUL LOVE STORY

"I will go," she said.
Genesis 24:58

WHEN THE TIME COMES FOR Isaac to marry, the responsibility to arrange an appropriate marriage falls to Abraham. He doesn't want his son to marry a pagan Canaanite girl, nor does he want Isaac to leave the Promised Land, where his future lies. Abraham, having learned firsthand of the pitfalls of moving away, sends his trusted servant back to his home country to find a suitable bride.

The servant's actions reflect a dependence on God—Abraham has taught his household well. The servant prays in a specific way so he will know which young woman he should choose. When Rebekah's father and brother are told of the way in which the prayer has been answered, they recognize that the event is more than coincidence. They do not object to the marriage, but leave the decision to Rebekah. They ask if she's willing to go to a faraway land and become the wife of a man she has never met. Without hesitation, she replies, "I will go" (Gen. 24:58).

Isaac and Rebekah love each other from the very beginning. Through their marriage, the family would continue its God-given destiny. Abraham, Isaac, and Jacob (the son of Isaac and Rebekah) become the patriarchs of the nation of Israel.

If we ask, God will lead us so that our desires and needs align with His plans for us and others. Following what God has already revealed through His Word and prayer gives us confidence in our choices and the courage to walk toward an unknown future.

COMPANION THOUGHT
Can you think of a time you did something unpredictable that you knew was the right thing to do? What gave you confidence?

Genesis 25
THE VALUE OF HERITAGE

Esau despised his birthright.
　　Genesis 25:34

AT ABRAHAM'S DEATH, THE LEGACY of faith passes to the next generation. Ishmael is included in Abraham's burial ritual. This gesture is the only kindness we see the family extend to Abraham's first son. It reminds us that as a child of Abraham born under special circumstances, Ishmael shares a legacy with Isaac. The son of Hagar will also become a great nation (Gen. 21:18).

Jacob's brother, Esau, has a unique place in God's story. His family has been chosen, rescued, and protected by God. God has given them great wealth and honor among their neighbors. Though Esau enjoys the advantages of this heritage, he does not appreciate them. In fact, he despises his birthright (Gen. 25:34).

Every person born into this world has a birthright—the gift of life. Innocence is another, for although we inherit Adam's inclination to sin, we are all born with a clean slate. Being created in God's image gives every human a right to dignity and liberty.

Most of us have received something of value from our parents. Even if our parents were difficult, even if they passed down things that hurt or limited us, we likely inherited abilities, interests, intellectual gifts, physical attributes, or character traits that have served us well. Any person brought up by parents who provided love, care, and support has indeed been blessed.

It is our responsibility to teach our children to value their spiritual heritage. Young ones follow our example, but they also need us to connect our actions to faith. Do our children understand why we make the choices we make? Do we help them see the benefits of knowing God? Faith is not a matter of "show or tell," but of "show *and* tell" (Deut. 11:19).

COMPANION THOUGHT
What is the modern equivalent of a "birthright"? Did you receive one? Did anyone else in your family?

Genesis 26

FAMILY VALUES

Isaac built an altar there and called on the name of the Lord.
    Genesis 26:25

GOD INTENDS THAT GODLY VALUES—BASIC moral codes for behavior—be passed from one generation to the other through the family. Isaac's life illustrates a well-known fact: traits of parents (both positive and negative) tend to be seen in their children. Character flaws that are not corrected often reoccur in following generations.

Years earlier to protect himself, Abraham had lied repeatedly about his wife, claiming she was his sister (Gen. 20:13). Now Abraham's son, Isaac, repeats the same sin. But Isaac also exhibits some of the family's positive traits. He calls on God and builds an altar, keeping himself in the flow of God's blessing. He obeys God, remaining in the land during famine. Like Abraham, he lives graciously, choosing to move on when conflicts arise rather than insist on his rights. Reclaiming his heritage, Isaac reopens wells that Abraham had dug in the past and forges ahead, digging new wells and guarding and and expanding the family's resources.

One grief is noted. Despite Isaac's obedience and God's blessing, Isaac's eldest son, Esau, continues to devalue his heritage by marrying pagan women (Gen. 26:34–35). We cannot choose God for our children. Even though they've been taught, some children choose the other way. But we should never give up. The great prophet Samuel, who grieved over God's disobedient people, said, "As for me, far be it from me that I should sin against the Lord by failing to pray for you" (1 Sam. 12:23). We keep praying for our lost children, refusing to let Satan take them. If we allow it, God will bring them to crisis points that give them the opportunity to repent and take their place in the family of God.

COMPANION THOUGHT

Is there someone in your family you're tempted to give up on? Why? Do you think God has given up on them?

Genesis 27

COSTLY MISTAKES

"Bless me too, my father!" Then Esau wept aloud.
Genesis 27:38

THE WRITER OF HEBREWS USES Esau as a warning to those who are careless about spiritual matters. "See that no one is sexually immoral, or is godless like Esau, who for a single meal sold his inheritance rights. . . . Afterward, as you know, when he wanted to inherit this blessing, he was rejected. Even though he sought the blessing with tears, he could not change what he had done" (Heb. 12:16–17).

For years, Esau placed no value on the blessing. By the time he changes his mind, his loss is irrecoverable. Does this mean we can never be forgiven for the sins of our past? No, but even though we repent and are forgiven, bad choices can cause us to lose relationships and opportunities that can never be regained. Like Esau, we cannot reverse the past. We can only repent and change the course of our lives so that we don't make the same mistakes again.

God is a God of many chances. It is never too late to start anew and let God bring good from all we've experienced. Acknowledging our sin and submitting ourselves to God places us where God can bless us, regardless of what we may have lost. "And we know that in all things God works for the good of those who love him, who have been called according to his purpose" (Rom. 8:28).

COMPANION THOUGHT

What's the difference between a wrongful act that has been forgiven and an irreversible consequence? Have you ever lost something irreplaceable?

JACOB (ISRAEL)

JACOB AND ESAU, THE TWIN sons born to Isaac and Rebekah, become symbols of opposite responses to faith: a life lived respecting God versus one that gives God no thought.

It's ironic that Jacob, who chooses a life of faith, struggles to conform his behavior to his deeply held beliefs. Jacob is one of the shabbiest persons of faith in Scripture. "Jacob" means "he grasps the heel" or "deceiver."[35] Isaac's younger son lives up to his name. Jacob spends his life fighting for what God has already determined to give him.

Jacob's life is one of conflict and contradictions. Though he places a high value on the family birthright and highly regards spiritual values, he is a schemer. He is always plotting against someone to get what he wants. He cheats his brother, Esau, out of the birthright and so angers him that Jacob must flee to keep Esau from killing him.

Yet despite Jacob's despicable flaws, God keeps reaching for him. The wonderful dream of the stairway going to heaven is an example of God's grace to an undeserving sinner.

There is a point when Jacob has a change of heart, a change of character, and a change of name. It is recorded in Genesis 32. God appears to Jacob and repeats the promise to make him a great nation. He then tells Jacob to return to the land of his father and grandfather. Jacob obeys, but is afraid. He sends his family, his livestock, and all he has across the river. Left alone, Jacob prays with more sincerity than he's ever prayed within his life. A man (later identified as God) comes and engages him in a wrestling bout.[36] The physical struggle is symbolic of the spiritual struggle between Jacob and the Lord. They wrestle throughout the night. Jacob will not let go until God blesses him. Near daybreak, the Lord permanently dislocates Jacob's hip, demonstrating that God could've disabled him at will. In the process, Jacob becomes a new man and receives a new name. He is no longer Jacob (meaning "deceiver") but Israel, which means "he struggles with God" (Gen. 32:28).[37]

Israel will become the name of the Jewish people. The descendants of Jacob become the Twelve Tribes of Israel.

Genesis 28
JACOB'S LADDER

He saw a stairway resting on the earth . . . reaching to heaven.
    Genesis 28:12

I T IS NO CREDIT TO Jacob that he is given a dream of such spiritual significance. He's a fugitive. The need for a wife gives him a pretext for leaving home. Isaac and Rebekah, upset that Esau has married outside the faith (and fearing Jacob may do the same), send Jacob to Harran, Rebekah's homeland. The truth is that having taken advantage of his brother's weakness, Jacob is now running for his life. It is hoped that Jacob's leaving will diminish Esau's anger.

Chosen by God (Rom. 9:10–13), Jacob did not need to resort to conniving and deceit. His actions now separate him from the very things he has been trying to secure—his place in the family, the land, his inheritance, and his future. Despite Jacob's continued refusal to trust, God gives him a glimpse of His plan to redeem the world. Jacob sees a stairway between heaven and earth from which God speaks. Of course, Jacob can't fully appreciate what this means. The stairway represents Jesus, the bridge between heaven and earth, whose death and resurrection will make direct access to God possible. Though Jacob's knowledge is limited, he senses the dream's truth—God is present, working in ways that are not visible to human eyes.

To Jacob, God reaffirms the same promises of land and descendants, of divine presence and protection, that he swore to Abraham and Isaac. Jacob's story is a beautiful example of God's faithfulness. God's promises depend on Him and are not voided by our shortcomings. "He who began a good work in you will carry it on to completion until the day of Jesus Christ" (Phil. 1:6).

COMPANION THOUGHT
Do you think it's possible for a person to have a change of heart and character? Do you know anyone who has?

I am with you and will watch over you wherever you go.
Genesis 28:15

Genesis 29

LABOR OF LOVE

Jacob was in love with Rachel.
    Genesis 29:18

IT IS LOVE AT FIRST sight. Jacob immediately wants the beautiful Rachel for his wife, but Rachel's father stands in his way. In Laban, Jacob meets his match. Laban deals with Jacob as treacherously as Jacob has dealt with others. Jacob agrees to work for his father-in-law seven years for Rachel, but those years "seemed like only a few days to him because of his love for her" (Gen. 29:20). The morning after the wedding, Jacob discovers he has not married Rachel, but her older sister, Leah. Jacob, who had deceived his father by pretending to be Esau, now feels what it's like to be on the other side of betrayal. Laban lets Jacob marry Rachel immediately, but requires Jacob to work another seven years for her.

The family dynamic Laban sets up pits Leah against Rachel, sister against sister, the loved against the unloved. The same pattern of jealousy that destroyed Jacob's relationship with his brother, Esau, takes root in Jacob's new family. In his birth family, Jacob was the instigator. In his new family, Jacob is the mediator. The rivalry between Rachel and her sister intensifies when four sons are born to Leah while Rachel remains barren.

God has a way of allowing circumstances in our lives to force us to deal with core character and behavioral issues. We can run away, but the problems that keep us from living with integrity will follow us. The Bible says, "Do not lose heart when he rebukes you, because the Lord disciplines the one he loves, and he chastens everyone he accepts as his son" (Heb. 12:5–6).

COMPANION THOUGHT
Do you have any rivalries in your family? Are they generational? How do they affect how you feel about God?

Genesis 30

JACOB'S THOUGHTS TURN TOWARD HOME

Send me on my way so I can go back to my own homeland.
Genesis 30:25

IT HAS BEEN TWENTY YEARS since Jacob left home. Jacob's relationship with his in-laws has been deteriorating, and after Rachel gives birth to a son, Jacob considers returning to his homeland. The problem is getting Laban to agree to a fair settlement. Jacob has worked hard and has prospered. He doesn't want to leave empty-handed. Given the nature of the two men, it is inevitable that the process of separation involves conniving and a battle of wits.

They agree on a plan for determining Jacob's share. Laban will take the white sheep. Jacob will take those that are speckled or dark. What transpires next isn't clear. Does Jacob know how to increase the number of speckled sheep through breeding techniques, or is he relying on superstition to manipulate the odds in his favor? Regardless, Jacob comes out ahead. When an unhappy Laban confronts him, Jacob accuses Laban of being unfair. Tensions mount as Jacob prepares to depart.

Both Laban and Jacob recognize that their prosperity is the result of God's blessing, yet they feel they must cheat, oppress, and manipulate to get ahead. Greed tears their family apart.

When God sees we are not willing to do things His way, He lets us persist in our destructive ways until we wear ourselves out or create a crisis. Jacob's story asks us to look closely at our struggles. Are they necessary? Are we worrying over what we cannot help or grasping for what God has already promised us? "Do not be anxious about anything, but in every situation, by prayer and petition, with thanksgiving, present your requests to God" (Phil. 4:6).

COMPANION THOUGHT
In this story, do you identify most with Jacob, Laban, Rachel, or Leah? Why?

Genesis 31

A PARTING BLESSING

May the Lord keep watch between you and me when we are away from each other.
 Genesis 31:49

AFTER REALIZING JACOB HAS LEFT in secret, Laban pursues and intends to retaliate, but in a dream, God tells him not to harm Jacob. The intervention should not be interpreted as God's approval of Jacob's actions. It means only that Laban is not the one to hold Jacob accountable.

We learn than Rachel (and we assume her household) does not worship God alone. She steals the family gods and lies about it, proving to be as skilled as her father and husband in deception (Gen. 31:30–35).

After a difficult interchange, Jacob and Laban come to terms. They make a covenant with each other and call upon God to be their witness in a ritual called Mizpah, meaning "watchtower."[38] Mizpah, though originating in a situation of mistrust, has become a prayer of blessing often used by family and friends who are going to be separated. Even in its original setting, this prayer, asking for God's watchful care, symbolizes reconciliation (Gen. 31:49).

Prayer can connect us to loved ones no matter how great the distance between us. We cannot always be present to share in their joys and sorrows, but God can. The Holy Spirit will guide us to pray for what they most need. "The Spirit intercedes for God's people in accordance with the will of God" (Rom. 8:27).

COMPANION THOUGHT
How can a blessing soften a parting? Think about using the Mizpah prayer with someone you love, and note what happens.

Genesis 32

JACOB WRESTLES WITH GOD

Jacob was left alone, and a man wrestled with him till daybreak.
Genesis 32:24

JACOB IS AFRAID. THE NEXT day, he will face his brother, Esau, who has vowed to kill him. Jacob can no longer hide from what he's done. Even more, he must come to grips with his relationship with God.

God comes to Jacob, challenging him physically, emotionally, and spiritually. The physical aspects of the incident are symbolic of the spiritual battle that has been going on for years—Jacob has been fighting against God. The man who is God in human form prevails.[39] Jacob is left with a permanent hip injury. Outwardly, he will limp for the rest of his life, but inwardly, he has been transformed. God gives him a new name. No longer will he be called Jacob ("deceiver"), but Israel, meaning "he struggled with God and with men and overcame" (Gen. 32:28).[40]

At last Jacob, now Israel, is ready to meet his brother.

God does not remove the struggles of our lives, He meets us in the midst of them. He comes when our greatest failures, deepest pain, and greatest fears have backed us into a corner. Desperation forces us to do what we've needed to do all along—have it out with God. A transforming encounter with the Lord enables us to face our future, however uncertain.

COMPANION THOUGHT
Have you ever had it out with God? Over what? What happened?

Genesis 33

THE REUNION

Esau ran to meet Jacob and embraced him; he threw his arms around his neck and kissed him. And they wept.

Genesis 33:4

FOR TWO DECADES, JACOB HAS worried about the day he would face Esau, and now it is here. We can almost hear Jacob's heart pounding as his brother approaches with a four-hundred-man army. Esau seems prepared for battle. Jacob has sent ahead a generous gift of livestock as a peace offering, but will Esau accept it? (Gen. 32:13). We can imagine Jacob's thoughts—*How can I make this right? Will Esau harm me and my family?* Jacob doesn't know that God has softened Esau's heart over the years. The work of God in one person's life often extends to the family.

Jacob and Esau reconcile. Ironically, God has given Jacob such wealth that the birthright—the double portion of wealth Jacob had obtained by taking advantage of his brother—is immaterial. Rather than take from Esau, Jacob now adds to his brother's wealth. God's provision is always extravagant and generous, much more than we can provide for ourselves.

As Jacob's mother isn't mentioned, it's likely Rebekah has died. The curse she called down on herself by deceiving Isaac came to pass (Gen. 27:13). She lost years she could've had with her beloved Jacob and his family. In Genesis. 35:29, we read of the peaceful end of Isaac's life: "Then [Isaac] breathed his last and died and was gathered to his people, old and full of years. And his sons Esau and Jacob buried him."

The death of our parents reminds us that life rushes by. If we are going to do things differently, this is the time. God says, "Forget the former things; do not dwell on the past. See, I am doing a new thing! Now it springs up; do you not perceive it?" (Isa. 43:18–19).

COMPANION THOUGHT

What reunions do you dread, and why? What is your favorite memory of a reunion with a distant friend or estranged family member? Was it better than expected?

Genesis 34

A TRAGEDY

Then Jacob said to Simeon and Levi, "You have brought trouble on me."
Genesis 34:30

MISTAKES MADE BY SEVERAL PEOPLE account for the tragic events in this chapter. Jacob settled near the city of Shechem and bought property there (Gen. 33:18–19). Following Lot's pattern, his family begins to associate with the people of Canaan. Dinah, who is allowed to venture into town without family protection, makes friends and meets a young man. Most versions say Shechem "took her" and "raped" her. Though this is God's and Jacob's family perspective, there's a possibility that Dinah was a willing participant (Gen. 34:3–4). Shechem speaks tenderly to Dinah and tries to negotiate a marriage. The Hebrew word translated "rape" means "humbled."[41] It includes sexual violence, but can also refer to a shaming event such as consensual sex outside of marriage. The couple may have had sexual relations to force their parents to approve a marriage they would otherwise deny.[42] Either rape or elopement would have brought shame to Jacob's family. The family is right to be outraged, but the brothers' revenge is out of proportion, and their violence places the entire family in danger (v. 30).

The outside world has always posed a threat to believers. While we are vulnerable to outright attacks on godly values, the subtle undermining of morality through associations we enjoy can be the greater problem. We live in tension in this life. We're not to isolate, and neither are we to identify or conform to the world's systems (Rom. 12:1–2). Proverbs 12:26 says, "The righteous choose their friends carefully, but the way of the wicked leads them astray."

COMPANION THOUGHT

Do you or a family member have a relationship with someone you're concerned about? What can you do to protect your family against that person's influence?

Genesis 35

BACK TO BETHEL

Come, let us go up to Bethel.
>   Genesis 35:3

BETHEL IS WHERE JACOB DREAMED of the stairway to heaven as he fled from Esau. It is where God assured him of His protection and presence. Now Jacob sees Bethel for the significant spiritual landmark that it is and obeys when God calls him to return. Before the journey, Jacob leads his family in a time of spiritual cleansing. Jacob's call to get rid of idols tells us he knew of their presence in the household and at least suspected they offended God (Gen. 35:2–5). The Ten Commandments have not yet been given, but Jacob's understanding that his family is to worship only the God of Abraham is growing. God reinforces Jacob's actions by answering his prayers for protection (v. 5).

At Bethel, God appears again to Jacob. After affirming Jacob's name change to Israel, He restates the promise of blessing to Jacob and his descendants. The passage notes that Jacob loses three people close to him: Rebekah's nurse, his beloved Rachel, and his father, Isaac. We don't know if weeks or years passed between Jacob's encounter with God at Bethel and these deaths, but Bethel must have given Jacob comfort and hope. He deals with his losses knowing that God's plan for his family continues (vv. 9–12).

Jacob's encounter with God reminds us there is value in connecting physical places to spiritual milestones. Do we remember where we've met God in a powerful way? Was it in a place we could claim as sacred? Perhaps a church, a room, or a place of nature? Have we thought to return to it, to bring our families with us and tell them our God stories? A spiritual landmark is not just a monument to the past; it can be "holy ground," a place where we and our children can go and experience God today.

COMPANION THOUGHT

Describe a place where something of spiritual significance happened to you. How did it impact you? Have you ever taken someone else there and told them the story?

Genesis 36

A GOOD MAN BUT WITHOUT GOD

Esau . . . moved to a land some distance from his brother Jacob. Their possessions were too great for them to remain together.
       Genesis 36:6–7

WHEN THE HERDS BELONGING TO Esau and Jacob become too large for the land to support, Esau gathers his family and possessions and relocates some distance away from his brother. The two men have coexisted for some time. Esau expresses no animosity against the family, but neither does he show any interest in the spiritual heritage of his ancestors.

Against his parent's wishes, Esau had chosen his wives from among the Hittites (Gen. 26:34). There is no mention of him calling on the Lord or building an altar to Him. Esau isn't a bad person. In many ways, he demonstrates better character than his brother, Jacob. However, though he is a good man, he is a man without God. Esau's move will take him even farther from the place where God is worshiped.

Esau is not excluded from God's blessings—he distances himself. There could have been a place for him, even though he was not the one through whom the promise would come. Sometimes our disappointment that life hasn't worked out as we hoped tempts us to walk away from God. But God and His gifts through His Son are always available to us. The choice is ours. "Everyone who calls on the name of the Lord will be saved" (Rom. 10:13).

COMPANION THOUGHT

Has there been a time when you've deliberately stepped away from God, the church, or your family? Why?

JOSEPH

THE EXPERIENCES JOSEPH ENDURES AS a young man would have broken most of us. He is sold into slavery by his brothers, falsely accused of rape by his employer's wife, unjustly sent to prison, and then forgotten by fellow prisoners whom he has befriended. Yet none of this embitters him. Holding to God, he continues to serve wherever he finds himself. In time, God vindicates him. Joseph the prisoner becomes the prime minister of Egypt, one of the mightiest nations in the world at that time.

Joseph's story receives more attention in Scripture than the story of any other person except Jesus. Though his life is documented in detail, nothing negative is written about him. Apart from his poor judgment as a youth (telling his brothers about his dreams), everything we know of Joseph is exemplary.

Joseph's treatment of his brothers reveals his character. He not only forgives them, but also offers his very dysfunctional family a chance to do things differently.

Joseph's faith in God never wavers. He remains positive, able to see God at work in both good and difficult times. He never loses sight of the promise God gave to Abraham, Isaac, and Jacob. Though Joseph brings the clan to Egypt, rescuing them from famine, he knows one day the family will return to the Promised Land. His dying request is that when the family does go back, they would take his bones with them. He wants to be buried in the land of promise. Four hundred years later, at the time of the exodus, Moses brings the bones of Joseph with him. As he desired, Joseph is buried in the tomb of his ancestors (Josh. 24:32).

Genesis 37

JOSEPH, THE BELOVED

Israel loved Joseph more than any of his other sons.
    Genesis 37:3

JOSEPH IS ONE OF THE few people in the Bible in whom we observe no major faults, no recorded moral failures, and no evidence of character flaw. His father Israel's blatant partiality toward Joseph causes his brothers to hate him. Joseph may have been foolish to tell his family about his dreams, but even that ultimately serves a good purpose. Later, when the dreams come to pass, Joseph's brothers and father recognize that God has been working out a plan all along.

The details Scripture gives of Joseph's family tell us family relationships are important in God's story and in our faith journey. Genesis highlights Joseph's family in all its glory and shame. From the start, the dysfunction of Jacob's (Israel's) blended family is remarkable, and yet God calls them to be the guardians of truth in the world.

The good news is that if God can redeem this family, He can redeem ours. The dynamics we witness in their story may feel close to home. Favoritism. Jealousy. Envy. Hate. Abuse. In this chapter, all that is wrong clouds God's promise, but God has miraculously preserved and strengthened the descendants of Abraham's family to this point. We read on, praying that God comes through for them and for us.

COMPANION THOUGHT

What's the worst thing that has happened in your family? Do you think it's possible for God to redeem that event?

Genesis 38
JUDAH—JOSEPH'S BROTHER

There Judah met the daughter of a Canaanite man.
Genesis 38:2

SCRIPTURE INTERRUPTS JOSEPH'S STORY WITH an account of Judah, one of Joseph's older brothers. Judah is important because the Messiah will come from his bloodline.

No attempt is made to gloss over Judah's sins. In fact, we can assume there are reasons for why this story is included in such detail. The first has to do with genealogy. Judah, who marries a Canaanite woman, has pagan offspring who are so wicked that God slays two of them (Gen. 38:7–10). We don't know if Judah's daughter-in-law, Tamar, is Canaanite or Jewish. Though Tamar's methods are questionable, she's determined to secure a place among God's people. She succeeds. One of Tamar's twins, Perez, will carry on the Messianic line.

Judah's choices serve as a warning. If our closest friends are unbelievers, we are easily drawn into situations and lifestyles incompatible with godly values. Every time Judah visits Hirah, the Adullamite, Judah ends up in trouble with a woman. The unsavory events recorded here warn us that when we compromise, people are hurt and our witness before the world is compromised.

Tamar's story also reminds us that God sees the powerless and works on their behalf. If we pursue God, neither our sins nor the sins of others can disqualify us from God's blessing. Whether we identify with Judah (the one who wronged another), Tamar (the one who was wronged), or Perez (the innocent victim), grace makes possible a place in God's family for all.

COMPANION THOUGHT

Is there a person who negatively influences you or someone in your family? How does this negative influence impact your family?

Genesis 39
RESISTING TEMPTATION

He . . . ran out of the house.
Genesis 39:12

JOSEPH WAS A "WELL-BUILT AND handsome" young man (Gen. 39:6). He seems to have inherited some of the features of his mother, Rachel, who "had a lovely figure and was beautiful" (Gen. 29:17). He is bright and evidently educated as he is quickly placed in authority in a high-ranking official's household. Joseph is pleasant, outgoing, and confident. Because God is with him, all he does prospers (Gen. 39:3).

Potiphar's wife is attracted to Joseph, and with his responsibilities in the house, she has ample opportunity to make advances. When she presses him, Joseph runs out of the house, leaving his cloak in her hand. Holding to his integrity, Joseph loses his position and his freedom and is sent to prison, but he doesn't allow injustice to eat away at him. In prison, he remains positive and finds opportunities to serve (v. 22).

Scripture describes Joseph as prosperous (successful) both in Potiphar's house and in prison. When God is with us, it doesn't matter where we are. He can cause us to flourish in any circumstance. And when God's Spirit rests on us, the world cannot help but notice. "The Lord was with Joseph and gave him success in whatever he did" (v. 23).

COMPANION THOUGHT

Have you ever paid a price to keep your integrity? What motivated you to make your choice? How do you feel about it now?

Genesis 40
POSITIVE EXPERIENCES IN PRISON

Tell me your dreams.
　　Genesis 40:8

JOSEPH IS INNOCENT, BUT DOESN'T become angry or bitter. Instead, he takes an interest in the people around him. Soon he's running the prison system, learning to navigate a large government bureaucracy. Unknown to him, God is preparing him for a task greater than anything he can imagine—the oversight of Egypt's food resources during a time of national crisis.

As Joseph waits in prison, the dreams of his fellow prisoners give him an opportunity to witness of God's power (Gen. 40:8). In ancient Near Eastern culture, dreams were believed to be reliable predictors of the future.[43] God works within this belief system for His own purposes. Confident of his close relationship with God, Joseph assures the baker and butler that God will show him the meaning of their dreams. God comes through. When events transpire as predicted, Joseph asks the butler to remember him to Pharaoh, but he forgets about Joseph.

When the deliverance we hope for does not come, and when the future we long for seems impossible, it's hard to keep trusting. We may resent the good that comes to others, especially if we've helped them make their way. Our perspective, however, is limited. We aren't privy to all God is doing. Perhaps His withholding what we desire for a season gives time for Him to do a greater work in our families, communities, and nations. As believers, we aren't to pursue what we want, but what God wants. He will give us peace as we wait. If what we hope for is delayed, we can be confident that God is at work behind the scenes (Rom. 8:28).

COMPANION THOUGHT
Have you ever had a recurring dream or nightmare? What do you think it means? Do you think God can speak to you through dreams?

Genesis 41
I CAN'T, BUT GOD CAN

"I cannot do it," Joseph replied to Pharaoh, "but God will give . . . the answer."
Genesis 41:16

AS A SLAVE AND A prisoner, Joseph has held to what he learned about God from his father, Jacob. God is all-powerful. He is a miracle worker.[44] Now standing before Pharaoh, Joseph is being called upon to do something beyond his ability. Pharaoh says, "I have heard it said of you that when you hear a dream you can interpret it" (Gen. 41:15). Joseph has no training in dreams like the wise men of Egypt, but Joseph knows the One who is the source of all knowledge and wisdom. God has revealed the meaning of dreams to him before,[45] but stakes are higher now. Failure in an interpretation could mean death. Do the words that the angel spoke to his great-grandmother, Sarah, come to his mind? "Is anything too hard for the Lord?" (Gen. 18:14). Joseph levels with Pharaoh: "I cannot do it, . . . but God will give Pharaoh the answer he desires" (Gen. 41:16).

Joseph does not find it awkward to talk to Pharaoh about the Lord. There is no hesitation or embarrassment. Joseph's heritage of faith and experience with God come through as naturally as breathing. He speaks, knowing God is with him.

Walking daily with the Lord makes it possible for us to endure hard times and maintain a godly witness with confidence. Past trials prepare us for the big moments. Is God orchestrating opportunities for us to make Him known? Is He opening doors? Do we have a heightened sense of His presence? God may be putting us in a place to "interpret" what He is doing for someone who seeking answers. The favor He gives us with our family, co-workers, church, communities, and governments are opportunities to proclaim God's truth with confidence.

COMPANION THOUGHT
Is anything too hard for God? Describe a time when God helped you speak with more clarity and authority than you expected.

Genesis 42
WEEPING FOR HIS BROTHERS

He turned away from them and began to weep.
     Genesis 42:24

JOSEPH TAKES ADVANTAGE OF THE fact that his brothers don't recognize him. He tests them. No doubt he wonders, *Will they stick together under pressure? Are they sorry for what they did to me years ago?*

Joseph loves his brothers. They connect him to his beloved aged father. They are his family, with whom he is linked past, present, and future. As he presses them, he is touched by the loyalty and concern the brothers show for each other. He learns that Reuben had intended to rescue him. As Joseph binds Simeon for prison (Simeon was the one who slaughtered Shechem and was likely the ringleader for wanting to kill Joseph), the distraught brothers acknowledge that this trouble is payback for their deeds. Joseph, reliving the betrayal of his brothers, is overcome with emotion. He flees behind closed doors and weeps.

Joseph shows wisdom in giving himself and his brothers time to come to terms with the cruel events. His brothers do not know that Joseph is alive, but at last they are dealing with their sin. We can only imagine what Joseph feels. He devises an elaborate plan that allows him to return their money and, he hopes, will force them to bring back his brother, Benjamin.

As Christians, we are told to forgive those who have wronged us, but Joseph's story shows us we can't sidestep grief. All losses deserve to be mourned. Jesus wept at the death of Lazarus, even though He would raise him up.[46] He wept in Gethsemane over the betrayals and suffering He would endure.[47] Grieving loss is a necessary step for healing, but we grieve with hope. With God, grief is not the end, but the beginning of something new.[48] The Lord "heals the brokenhearted and binds up their wounds" (Ps. 147:3).

COMPANION THOUGHT
What past trouble would you like God to help you "forget"? How is betrayal a loss? How can you grieve it?

Genesis 43
AMAZING GRACE

Your God, the God of your father, has given you treasure in your sacks.
    Genesis 43:23

GRACE—UNMERITED FAVOR—IS ONE OF THE great themes of Scripture. Here, in the first book of the Old Testament, grace is highlighted in the Joseph narrative. His story gives us an in-depth look at grace in the place we most often fail to give it, in the place where it is most needed—the family.

Joseph begins with a practical gift. The brothers of Joseph have purchased grain with the appropriate amount of silver. Yet to their amazement, they discover their silver in their sack, along with the grain. Joseph's brothers do not deserve the money.

Joseph's steward tells them God has given them the silver, and in a sense, He has. Though the Lord often works through people, God is the source of every blessing (James 1:17). Joseph is working toward giving his brothers a greater gift than silver—forgiveness. He isn't there yet, but in showing kindness and generosity, he begins to walk down that path.

If we find it hard to forgive another, we can start by taking one small step. As we move forward, the next step toward forgiveness becomes possible. In time, God will empower us to give to others the same grace He's given to us. Jesus taught us to pray,, "Forgive us our debts, as we also have forgiven our debtors" (Matt. 6:12). As we set others free, Christ frees us from the grief, anger, and hurt that have crippled us.

COMPANION THOUGHTS
Is there someone you need to forgive? Can you think of a gift or act of kindness that could help you do it?

Genesis 44

A MISTAKEN ASSUMPTION

His brother is dead, and he is the only one of his mother's sons left.
   Genesis 44:20

JUDAH ASSUMES JOSEPH IS DEAD. It is a likely assumption. Slaves usually did not survive many years because of the harsh treatment they received. Judah doesn't realize that the very person to whom he is now speaking—the prime minister of Egypt—is his brother.

Our assumptions are often mistaken. We seldom have all the facts, and we fail to put God into the equation. Before we write people off, we should consider the power of God. Long after we give up, God continues to work, often in ways beyond what we hope for.

Our word to Judah would be: "Do not say Joseph is dead. He has been away for a long time, but he is alive and well. He will be given back to you and will bring blessing to you and your family."

We never know what the Lord will do in our lives and in the lives of those around us. "With God all things are possible" (Matt. 19:26). What we think is dead, God can bring to life. What we think is lost, He can restore.

COMPANION THOUGHT
What is something you thought was gone forever that God has restored?

Genesis 45

GOD WORKS FOR OUR GOOD

It was not you who sent me here, but God.
    Genesis 45:8

JOSEPH IS NOT JUST BEING kind to his brothers to ease their guilt; he is honestly expressing his perspective of the events that have happened. "It was not you who sent me here, but God" (Gen. 45:8). Joseph's words help his family see that God has used everything from the past to save them. The pit, slavery, prison—they were all folded into God's plan. Joseph's trials refined and groomed him for leadership. The brothers' guilt over abusing Joseph leads to their repentance. God is honored in the courts of Egypt, and the family God has chosen to carry His story forward in the world is preserved.

A mystery of God's providence is that He can use the evil of life to accomplish His purposes. Evil deeds are not excused, and those who commit them will be held accountable—but God can redeem anything, even the wrongdoings of others.

A touching aspect of Joseph's story is God's personal care for Joseph. The safeguarding of His people is not God's only concern. By exalting Joseph to a position of power, God vindicates him before those who had meant him harm. We are not expendable pawns in God's plans—we are His beloved. God not only cares about His kingdom and His church, He cares about us. "Cast your cares on the Lord and he will sustain you; he will never let the righteous be shaken" (Ps. 55:22).

COMPANION THOUGHT

Do you feel as if your feelings and concerns don't matter? Why? What good can come from the pain you've experienced?

I am God, the God of your father," he said. "Do not be afraid..."
Genesis 46:3

Genesis 46

A DIFFICULT DECISION

God spoke to Israel . . . , "Do not be afraid to go down to Egypt. . . . I will go down to Egypt with you, and I will surely bring you back again."
Genesis 46:2–4

JACOB GRAPPLES WITH JOSEPH'S INVITATION to go to Egypt. Going will affect Jacob's family long-term. No doubt he's afraid the clan will suffer. Perhaps he worries that moving to Egypt is a compromise. God's promises are linked to the land of Canaan. In the last great famine, God had told his father, Isaac, not to leave (Gen. 26:2). Jacob wants nothing, not even the compelling economic pressure or the unusual family circumstances, to distance him from God's blessing and the covenant.

In the depth of his struggle, Jacob receives a message from God. In a vision, God tells him to go to Egypt. He assures Jacob that He will make a great nation of him there and will eventually bring the family back to Canaan. Knowing that God is leading him, Jacob agrees to the move. He spends his last days near his beloved Joseph.

Guidance must be discerned through our daily walk with God. He expects us to know His truth and to use the minds and free will He has given us to make life choices. But at critical junctures, God may call us to something new, perhaps something different others will not understand. If we listen, God will direct us. "Whether you turn to the right or to the left, your ears will hear a voice behind you, saying, 'This is the way; walk in it'" (Isa. 30:21).

COMPANION THOUGHT
What choice have you made that other people haven't understood? Who would you like to live near in your old age? Why?

Genesis 47

TAKE ME TO THE PROMISED LAND

Do not bury me in Egypt, but when I rest with my fathers, carry me out of Egypt and bury me where they are buried.
Genesis 47:29–30

NEAR DEATH, JACOB REQUESTS THAT his body be returned to the land of his fathers for burial. Egypt has been good to him. In Egypt, he has been united with Joseph, and Pharaoh has been kind to him and his family. They have all prospered. But Jacob's heart is in the land God promised to him and his descendants. Jacob knows that his family's sojourn in Egypt is temporary. Egypt is not their home. His family is destined to become a great nation, and the future of that nation is in Canaan, not in Egypt. Jacob's desire to be buried in Canaan shows that neither years nor distance have diminished his faith.

In the symbolism of Scripture, Egypt is a type of the world. It represents a society of people without God. As believers, we are called to engage fully in the place to which God calls us. But as we raise our families, work, and serve, we are to keep the long view in mind. Our home is with God. Even the Promised Land, as important as it is in anchoring faith to God in Israel's history, is not a final destination. Canaan points to the eternal kingdom revealed in Jesus. The apostle Paul would later explain, "But our citizenship is in heaven. And we eagerly await a Savior from there, the Lord Jesus Christ" (Phil. 3:20).

COMPANION THOUGHT

Where is your family home? Are you attached to it?

Genesis 48

JACOB IMPARTS THE "BLESSING"

Then he blessed Joseph.
   Genesis 48:15

THE JACOB WHO BLESSES HIS sons is not the same man who wrested the blessing from his brother so many years before. His role as guardian of the faith has been costly, but he's learned that God controls his family's destiny. Now it is time for Jacob to pass leadership to the next generation. In Old Testament times, this was done through the ritual of the blessing.[49]

Because of a moral indiscretion, Reuben, Jacob's firstborn son, forfeits the birthright (Gen. 49:3–4).[50] Jacob gives it to Joseph instead. After formally adopting Joseph's two sons, Jacob gives each of them a portion among his own sons. The spiritual blessing goes to Ephraim and Manasseh as well. In the future listings of the twelve tribes, Levi is not listed. Later, God chooses the tribe of Levi to be priests and they will not inherit land (Deut. 18:1–2).[51] Neither is Joseph listed. Ephraim and Manasseh represent his lineage. (These descendants of Jacob become the Twelve Tribes of Israel: Reuben, Simeon, Judah, Dan, Naphtali, Gad, Asher, Issachar, Zebulun, Manasseh, Ephraim, and Benjamin.)

Though Joseph had received the inheritance of a firstborn despite his birth order, he objects as Jacob begins to confer the greater blessing to Joseph's younger son, Ephraim (Gen. 48:17–18). Joseph wants his father to observe tradition. But Jacob, who'd been the younger, continues the pattern begun with him and Esau. In the New Testament "the younger serving the older" becomes symbolic of God's sovereignty and grace. God's favor is not given based on our own standing, but simply because God chooses us. "It does not, therefore, depend on human desire or effort, but on God's mercy" (Rom. 9:16).

COMPANION THOUGHT

Do you feel you have the blessing of your parents? What blessing would you like to give to your children?

Genesis 49

THE LION OF THE TRIBE OF JUDAH

The scepter will not depart from Judah.
Genesis 49:10

IN JACOB'S FAREWELL ADDRESS, HE speaks personal words to each of his sons. He notes striking character traits—some positive, some negative—and then gives an appraisal of the man and his family group. Jacob's words are based on his knowledge of each son. In ancient Near Eastern culture, a father's solemn utterances at life's end were significant. Jacob's sons would have understood Jacob's words as having power to influence their individual and family destinies.[52]

Judah, the fourth son by Leah, is the first to receive unqualified praise. Though he has no special birthright or spiritual advantage, Jacob predicts Judah will emerge as the family's leader. He describes Judah as exerting power and leadership over all the others. "Judah, your brothers will praise you; . . . your father's sons will bow down to you. You are a lion's cub. . . . The scepter will not depart from Judah" (Gen. 49:8–10). Jacob refers to Judah as a lion. The same theme is picked up in Revelation 5:5 as the writer says of Jesus, "See, the Lion of the tribe of Judah, the Root of David, has triumphed." Jesus is of the tribe of Judah.

Words can build up or destroy. They can affirm, they can help us put past hurts into perspective, or they can crush. They can free us, or they can imprison us in our past and undermine our future. Jacob's parting words do all these things at various times. While his assessments of his sons may have been accurate, Jacob shows little grace toward those who faltered. We can learn from the mistakes of this patriarch who, though chosen of God, offers little comfort or hope for his wayward children. "The Lord is compassionate and gracious, slow to anger, abounding in love" (Ps. 103:8).

COMPANION THOUGHT

What is the best thing you remember your parents saying about you? The worst? How did their words shape who you are?

You intended to harm me, but God intended it for good.
Genesis 50:20

Genesis 50
JOSEPH REASSURES HIS BROTHERS

Don't be afraid. I will provide for you and your children.
    Genesis 50:21

AFTER THEIR FATHER'S DEATH, THE brothers fear that Joseph will retaliate for the way they had treated him. But Joseph reassures his brothers. He urges them not to be afraid, giving them one of the most powerful perspectives of God's sovereignty found in Scripture: "You intended to harm me, but God intended it for good to accomplish what is now being done, the saving of many lives" (Gen. 50:20).

We know Joseph believed this. His actions prove it. Joseph not only provided for his brothers and their families, but "He reassured them and spoke kindly to them" (Gen. 50:21). However, forgiveness does not mean we abolish all boundaries. Joseph continued to live in the city, away from his family. Physical distance allowed him to maintain a healthy relationship. Joseph dies as he lived—confident that God would fulfill all His promises. Faith that God will continue to bring good out of evil gives Joseph freedom to love those who had hurt him.

Guarding our emotional stability while staying vulnerable requires the discernment of the Holy Spirit. The Holy Spirit both empowers us to extend kindness and grace to those who do not deserve it and helps us maintain appropriate boundaries. Our genesis—our new beginning—comes through faith. Faith takes us beyond the limitations of our family or our circumstances. Faith invites us into God's world, where His promises and blessings await us. "So those who rely on faith are blessed along with Abraham, the man of faith" (Gal. 3:9).

COMPANION THOUGHT
Have you ever forgiven someone who couldn't accept it? Have you ever rejected the forgiveness someone else has offered you? How did you deal with it?

JOSEPH AS A TYPE OF CHRIST

THE OLD TESTAMENT GIVES US glimpses of the kind of Messiah Jesus will be through people who reflect God's character or share Jesus's life experiences. There are many similarities between Joseph and Jesus. Each man:

- Was beloved by his father (Gen. 37:3; Matt. 3:17).
- Was rejected by his family (Gen. 37:8–9; John 1:11).
- Was delivered to the gentiles (Gen. 37:26; John 18:28).
- Was severely tempted (Gen. 39:7; Matt. 4:1).
- Was taken to Egypt (Gen. 37:26; Matt. 2:14–15).
- Was stripped of his robe (Gen. 37:23; John 19:23–24).
- Was sold for the price of a slave (Gen. 37:28; Matt. 26:15).
- Was falsely accused (Gen. 39:16–18; Matt. 26:59–60).
- Was with two other prisoners—one lost, one saved (Gen. 40:2–3; Luke 23:32).
- Stood before rulers (Gen. 41; John 18).
- Possessed power acknowledged by authorities (Gen. 41:38; John 19:19).
- Saved those who sought to kill him (Gen. 50:29; Luke 23:24).
- Was highly exalted after suffering (Gen. 41:41; Phil. 2:9–10).
- Fed the hungry (Gen. 41:46–57; Matt. 14:13–21).
- Had others bow before him (Gen. 42:5–7; Phil. 2:10–11).
- Forgave and restored those who betrayed him (Gen. 45:1–15; John 21:15–17).

THE BOOK OF EXODUS

AT THE END OF GENESIS, the Israelites have settled in Egypt as the honored family of the capable and beloved prime minister, Joseph. They've prospered and multiplied, but four hundred years and a series of political events have reversed their fortunes. A new pharaoh sees their growing numbers as a threat. Needing a labor force for his building projects, he enslaves the children of Israel.[53]

The book of Exodus recounts the dramatic liberation of the Israelites from Pharaoh's rule. The word *exodus* means "a mass departure: emigration."[54] Under the leadership of Moses, the Israelites travel toward Canaan to possess the land God promised to Abraham some five hundred years before.

The descendants of Jacob leave Egypt as a tribal group of slaves, but along the way become a nation. As the Israelites face the impossible task of claiming their inheritance, God uses hardships, isolation, and even the sins of the people to teach them who He is and to forge their identity as His people.

Exodus is the second of the first five books of the Old Testament called the Pentateuch. The historical events described in these books (also referred to as the *Books of Moses*) form the religious, political, social, and cultural foundation of the Hebrew nation.[55] Like most of the Old Testament, the Books of Moses are told from a third-person, omniscient point of view in which the author knows what everyone is thinking.[56] This viewpoint, a characteristic of Hebrew storytelling, makes it sound as though God Himself tells the story.[57] Second Timothy 3:16 tells us, "All Scripture is God-breathed." The author who "knows all and sees all" reinforces our understanding that the Bible is God's Word and can be trusted.

The Pentateuch is filled with symbols of the Christian faith that are explained in the New Testament, such as the exodus (deliverance from sin), Passover (blood for the atonement of sin), the Law (the call to righteous living), the Levite priests (a mediator for sin), and the Holy of Holies (God's holiness and presence). These symbols come to life in the person of Jesus Christ.

The book of Exodus covers three defining events:

1. The *exodus* of the Israelites from Egypt (chapters 1–18).
2. The giving of the *Law* on Mount Sinai (chapters 19–24).
3. The construction of the *tabernacle* (chapters 25–40).

The *exodus*. The exodus remains the most important event in Israel's history. Thousands of years later, the Jewish people still celebrate their deliverance from Egyptian bondage with an annual celebration called Passover. Jesus linked the Passover to Himself, making His life, death, and resurrection the defining historical event for Christians. On the night before His death, Jesus modified the ancient Passover feast to create the ritual we now observe as the Lord's Supper. Communion identifies Jesus Christ as the Passover lamb.[58]

The *Law*. The commands God gives to Moses at Mount Sinai teach the people the difference between holy and unholy. Awareness that God is holy and must be respected as such is essential to having a relationship with Him. The Law brings God into everyday life and sets the standard for how we are to relate to God and each other.

The *tabernacle*. The ingenious portable worship center God designs leads us to the theme of the book—the presence of God.[59] The tabernacle becomes Yahweh's symbolic home, a sign that He dwells in the midst of His people. The tabernacle (the forerunner of the temple) houses the stop-gap system of animal sacrifice for the forgiveness of sins that will remain until Jesus comes.

Exodus records historic events from a divine perspective,[60] yet it is more than history. It lays the groundwork for understanding Jesus's sacrifice, yet it is more than symbols. The book of Exodus gives us a deeper understanding of Yahweh as a relational God. We learn that God is powerful, but not impersonal.[61] He loves His people and wants to live among them. From the exodus on, the children of Israel will be known as God's special people (Ex. 6:7).

Like the New Testament, Exodus teaches that the Law is not the means of salvation, but is a guide for maintaining our relationship with God.[62] The book of Exodus stretches our faith, daring us to believe that God not only can, but also will, deliver us from sin. Exodus tells us that God's plans cannot be stopped by any human force. It shows us that God is holy and we are not; if we want to stay in relationship with Him, we must deal with our sin. In Exodus, we see that the desire of God's heart is to be present among us. "I will take you as my own people, and I will be your God" (Ex. 6:7).

Exodus 1
TOUGH TIMES FOR GOD'S PEOPLE

The more they were oppressed, the more they multiplied and spread.
    Exodus 1:12

THE CONCLUDING STATEMENT OF GENESIS becomes the starting point of Exodus—what others intended for harm, God uses for good (Gen. 50:20). Pharaoh's abuse, though crushing and unfair, prepares the enslaved Israelites for their freedom. Making and hauling bricks makes them strong and physically fit. The harshness of their conditions makes them willing to take risks for freedom.

Historically, Christianity has flourished in difficult times. The persecution of the church in the first century sparked such growth that Tertullian, an early church apologist, noted, "The blood of the martyrs is the seed of the church."[63]

The very things that are unfair in life strengthen us. The Bible challenges us to believe that with God as our protector and provider, our future is brighter than we can imagine. Freedom is both an event (a moment when we are delivered) and a journey. Exodus is our opportunity to travel with God, to be set free from sins and behaviors that enslave us, and to be amazed by God as He transforms trouble into triumph.

The Bible says, "Consider it pure joy, my brothers and sisters, whenever you face trials of many kinds, because you know that the testing of your faith produces perseverance. Let perseverance finish its work so that you may be mature and complete, not lacking anything" (James 1:2–4).

COMPANION THOUGHT
What is the most difficult move you've made in your life? Why?

MOSES

MOSES, BORN OF HEBREW SLAVE parents, is adopted by an Egyptian princess when he is three months old. He grows up as royalty, but maintains a relationship with his birth family.[64] His mother and father must have believed in the promises of God, as all three of their children—Moses, his brother, Aaron, and his sister, Miriam—exhibit strong faith. Together, the trio leads the emerging nation in the worship of Yahweh. The book of Hebrews tells us that from an early age, Moses identifies with the Israelites (Heb. 11:23–29).

Moses's passion for his people may explain why he is at a Hebrew worksite and why he kills an Egyptian he sees abusing an Israelite (Ex. 2:11–15). When the murder becomes known, Moses flees to the desert. Moses's impulsive act costs him his privileged life and the opportunity to help his people. Moses lives as a nomadic shepherd in Midian, all the education and leadership training he had received in Pharaoh's court seemingly wasted. But one day God appears to Moses in a burning bush and gives the fugitive an impossible task: Moses is to free the Hebrews from Egyptian bondage and lead them to Canaan, the land God has promised them (Ex. 3).

Moses objects, claiming he's a poor speaker (Ex. 4:10). It has been suggested he has a speech impediment,[65] but it's possible Moses is uneasy speaking publicly because of his multicultural upbringing. Shuttled between his Hebrew family and the Egyptian court, Moses may have struggled to express himself well in either language. It is also likely Moses had been speaking a dialect of Hebrew in Midian for forty years.[66] The thought of addressing Hebrew and Egyptian leaders must have been terrifying to him. Failure could mean hardship or death for him and God's people. God responds by appointing Aaron as Moses's spokesperson.

At first, Aaron does speak for Moses, but as God begins to reveal Himself through the plagues, Moses gains confidence. Moses announces the seventh plague and from then on, takes the lead (Ex. 9).

At the burning bush, God had promised to be with Moses's mouth (Ex. 4:11–12). When Moses surrenders to God, his weakness becomes a strength. Acts 7:22 says Moses was "powerful in speech and action." Scripture portrays Moses as a gifted, poetic orator and a persuasive advocate.

Moses has his share of human frailties. Anger proves a lifetime struggle. Yet he has many strengths. An organized, humble, capable leader, Moses not only possesses the practical skills to survive in the desert, but also proves to be a strong political and military commander. His greatest asset is his spiritual leadership. Like other giants of Scripture, Moses encounters God in a dramatic way. "The Lord would speak to Moses face to face, as one speaks to a friend" (Ex. 33:11). The shepherd who once hid his face from the burning bush becomes consumed with knowing God (Ex. 33).

Under Moses's leadership, God's people walk away from slavery and begin a journey that will take them to Canaan, the land God has promised them. Soon after a miraculous crossing of the Red Sea, God gives Moses the Law. The Law not only lays down principles of righteous living, but also teaches the people that God is holy, just, and merciful. As they travel to the Promised Land, Moses helps the people understand that how they live determines whether they experience God's blessing or discipline. Moses keeps the Israelites on track and intercedes for them when they falter. The Hebrews arrive in Canaan as a free and mighty nation. Their presence testifies of God's power to rescue, guide, and protect. Early on, Moses grasps that God is making Himself known to the nations[67] and exhorts the children of Israel to honor God and serve Him.[68]

Today, no one thinks of Moses as the Egyptian prince. Instead, we remember him as the great Hebrew leader who led God's people out of Egypt. Moses is not only one of the most important men of the Old Testament, but he is one of the greatest leaders who ever has lived.

Exodus 2
A CAREER-ENDING MISTAKE

He killed the Egyptian and hid him in the sand.
      Exodus 2:12

THE MURDER OF THE EGYPTIAN ends Moses's promising career as a national leader. Moses runs to the desert, where he joins a nomadic family in Midian. They refer to Moses as "an Egyptian" (Ex. 2:19). It seems Moses no longer identifies with the people of God. As a shepherd, Moses learns to thrive in the desert, yet he names his son Gershom, meaning "exile" or "stranger."[69] Moses is resigned to his life in Midian, but Midian isn't home. Just as we think Moses's story has come to an end, we learn that events in Egypt have God's attention. God sees the Israelites suffering and remembers He made a covenant with Abraham and his descendants (vv. 23–25). We sense that Moses's destiny is still tied to the Hebrews.

The gap between Moses's hope for his people and God's promise is enormous. Even if Moses had won better working conditions for his people, they still would have been slaves. For the Hebrews to inherit the land of Canaan, they would have to be free. Impossible. The chapter ends unsettled, but with hope. Does God intend to do something for Moses? For the Israelites?

We may think our lives are over. Perhaps we've blown our families or ministries apart. We may feel exiled. Finished. But our vision is too small. We want relief from current circumstances, but God wants our freedom. Our mistakes and sins prove we cannot do God's work on our own. Jesus says, "Apart from me you can do nothing" (John 15:5). It may take failure and years for us to realize, but once we do, then God begins His liberating work. Our "ending" is God's "beginning."

COMPANION THOUGHT
Have you ever stepped back from your family or ministry? Why?

Exodus 3
MOSES AT THE BURNING BUSH

God called to him from within the bush, "Moses! Moses!" And Moses said, "Here I am."
Exodus 3:4

MOSES'S ANSWER, "HERE I AM," suggests a willingness to be available to God (Ex. 3:4). But when Moses learns what God is asking him to do, he backpedals. Chapter three and most of chapter four consist of Moses arguing with God. Moses is through with the Israelite people and is through with Egypt. "Who am I that I should go to Pharaoh and bring the Israelites out of Egypt?" he asks (Ex. 3:11). His fancy education and royal status had led him nowhere. What's different now? God answers him, "I will be with you" (v. 12).

God's presence makes all the difference. We see this in the biblical accounts of great leaders such as Abraham, Moses, Gideon, Isaiah, and Paul.[70] Most of them had little to show for their efforts before encountering God. Only when they surrender to God do they accomplish anything of lasting value. Even then, the reality and timing look nothing like what they envisioned.

We may wonder why God has given us a love for certain peoples, nations, languages, music, art, and vocations, yet has not allowed us to reap anything but disappointment. Trusting in God's sovereignty and timing becomes our statement of faith. God reminds us that He is the I Am, the God of Abraham, Isaac, and Jacob, the God of the covenant (v. 14). When God goes with us, we can rest knowing that in His time, all the promises He has made to us will come to pass. The impossible is possible.

COMPANION THOUGHT
Describe a time when you felt you were on holy ground. How did it change you?

Exodus 4

UNDERESTIMATED RESOURCES

What is that in your hand?
    Exodus 4:2

MOSES'S RESPONSE TO GOD AT the burning bush isn't what we'd expect. The expelled prince raises objections. As Moses ticks off his *what ifs*, he seems to be making excuses rather than seeking honest answers. "What if Pharaoh won't listen to me? What if the Israelites don't believe you've sent me? What if . . . " God halts the questions with one of His own: "What is that in your hand?" (Ex. 4:2). The answer is obvious. Moses holds a common shepherd's staff. But God will use a staff to convince a despot to free His people, to part the Red Sea, and to provide water in the desert.[71] But first, Moses must experience the power of God Himself. In the desert, alone with God, he throws down his staff as God commands, and it becomes a snake. When he takes it by the tail, the snake becomes a rod again (vv. 3-4).

We all have resources that God can use. We tend to underestimate our talents and gifts, failing to recognize that God can work miracles through them. What's in our hand? A skill? Financial resources? A good mind? A measure of health? Time? Our family? A network? A talent? To symbolically "throw down" the resources God has given us (v. 3), we give God's gifts back to Him. We let them go. What we surrender, God transforms and uses to reveal who He is to us and to the world.

COMPANION THOUGHT
What do you see as your greatest strength? Do any of your gifts cause problems in relating to others? How?

Exodus 5

WHEN THINGS DON'T WORK OUT

Why, Lord, why have you brought trouble on this people?
    Exodus 5:22

IN OBEDIENCE TO GOD'S CALL, Moses returns to Egypt, but nothing is working out as planned. Pharaoh refuses to let God's people go and retaliates against the already overburdened Hebrews. The people turn on Moses.

Moses cries out, "Why, Lord, why have you brought trouble on this people? Is this why you sent me? . . . You have not rescued your people at all" (Ex. 5:22–23).

Moses's desperate circumstances leave no other alternative than to depend upon God. In the New Testament, we read of Paul reaching a similar point. He had a "thorn in the flesh" that God refused to remove (2 Cor. 12:7–9). Exhausted from ministry and seeing no relief in sight, Paul despaired of life (2 Cor. 1:8). God's answer to Paul and to anyone in desperate circumstances is, "My grace is sufficient for you, for my power is made perfect in weakness" (2 Cor. 12:9).

If God allowed Moses and Paul to be severely tested, should we be surprised when He tests our faith and endurance? In Scripture, no person is greatly used of God without a period of testing. Even Jesus was tested. Immediately before launching His public ministry, Jesus endured forty days of intense temptation in the wilderness (Matt. 4:1–11). The test is never the end; it is the means of strengthening faith (James 1:2–4).

When life seems the opposite of what God has promised us, we can run to God. He listens, letting us vent our fears and disappointments while we wait for Him to rescue. The Lord will sustain us, and when the time is right, He will act.

COMPANION THOUGHT

Have you ever been the scapegoat for someone else's anger? How did you handle it?

Exodus 6

"I AM . . . I WILL"

I am the Lord, and I will bring you out. . . . I will free you. . . . I will redeem you. . . . I will take you as my own people, and I will be your God.
Exodus 6:6–7

JUST WHEN MOSES IS READY to give up, the Lord instructs him to tell the people to get ready—He is going to deliver them and give them the land He'd promised to Abraham. For four hundred years, God's people have waited for this news.

But when it comes, they reject it. Although God is reaffirming His covenant to the Israelites, their anguish blinds them to God's gift. In retrospect, we see a purpose in the trials: they make clear that Yahweh—not Moses—is their Savior. But at the time, the circumstances seem disastrous.

Moses enlists the help of his brother, Aaron, a respected leader of the Levites, to gather the clans (Ex. 6:25). Moses relays the message of deliverance God had given to him (vv. 6–8). Three times God had said, "I am." Seven times He said, "I will." But because the Hebrews do not know who Yahweh is, they don't believe His promises. The tribal leaders hear out Moses, but do not change their minds (v. 9). The genealogy in verses 13–26 confirms that as direct descendants of Abraham, Moses and Aaron have authority to claim the covenant. Despite lack of support, God instructs them to proceed with His plan: they must tell Pharaoh to let God's people go.

Faith requires some understanding of who God is. We must be patient with those who know little about the Lord and pray they learn of Him through us. If their pain is so great that they can't hear God speak, God may send us to stand beside them for a season and believe on their behalf. No matter what others do, we are to keep moving forward in faith, proclaiming who God is. "But you are a chosen people, a royal priesthood, a holy nation, God's special possession, that you may declare the praises of him who called you out of darkness into his wonderful light" (1 Peter 2:9).

COMPANION THOUGHT

Do you tend to be skeptical when someone promises you something? Why or why not?

HEBREW STORYTELLING IN SCRIPTURE

TYPICALLY, HEBREW STORIES HAVE THE following characteristics:[72]

- **Omniscient narrator.** Stories are told by an anonymous third-person narrator who sees all and knows all.
- **"Show," not "tell."** Speech and actions reveal plot and character. We learn who the characters are and what they are like by what they say and do. If we're told what someone is like, it's important.
- **Sparse physical descriptions.** If details are given, they're significant to the story.
- **Motivations seldom stated.** Motives must be deduced from conversations and behavior.

In Scripture, we can't assume that everything a "good" person does is good or that all a "bad" person does is bad. We must discern whether God approves or disapproves of the person's behavior based on what the Bible says. The Bible not only tells us what God says, but it also alerts us to Satan's schemes and lies. We are to "test the spirits to see whether they are from God, because many false prophets have gone out into the world" (1 John 4:1). Hebrew storytelling in the Bible requires us to do what we must do in life—apply God's Word to distinguish between His ways and the ways of the world.

Exodus 7
LET MY PEOPLE GO

Let my people go, so that they may worship me.
    Exodus 7:16

IN CHAPTER 5, MOSES ASKED Pharaoh for permission to take the Israelites into the desert to worship God. But God's intent from the start is to lead His people out of Egypt. Is He instructing Moses to lie, or is Moses giving Pharoah a chance to save face? From their exchange, it seems both Pharaoh and Moses understand that the real issue is the release of the Hebrews from Egypt. Once the Hebrews leave, they will not return.

Yet Pharaoh refuses to let God's people go. Hebrew slave labor is a vital part of Egypt's economy, an asset he's unwilling to relinquish. He will soon learn he has no choice. Pharaoh's opponent is not Moses, but the One True God the Hebrews call Yahweh.

God says the Israelites will go, and by the time they leave, "the Egyptians will know that I am the Lord" (Ex. 7:5). Ten plagues come upon the Egyptians in succession. Some biblical interpreters suggest these plagues challenge the Egyptian gods.[73] The Nile is the first deity to be humiliated as God turns the water to blood. Yet Pharaoh does not give in.

God may reveal Himself to us by stripping away what we most trust. He will use life events to get our attention until we have no choice but to acknowledge that He is God. We can resist God, but we will not prevail. Isaiah 45:9 says, "Woe to those who quarrel with their Maker. . . . Does the clay say to the potter, 'What are you making?'" When we understand that God has authority over us, we will not demand, but surrender. "Yet you, Lord, are our Father. We are the clay, you are the potter; we are all the work of your hand" (Isa. 64:8).

COMPANION THOUGHT
Can you think of a time when being less than honest seemed the right thing to do? What was your motive? Who benefited most?

Exodus 8

THE PLAGUES

If you refuse to let them go, I will send a plague of frogs on your whole country.
Exodus 8:2

GOD CONTINUES TO PRESS PHARAOH to release the Hebrews. The first plague had so polluted the Nile that it couldn't sustain life. Now frogs abandon the river and swarm over the land. These frogs are the second of the ten plagues.

Many of the disasters related to the plagues were not uncommon in the region. Some Bible scholars believe the plagues were accelerated natural disasters.[74] Whether this was the case or not, the plagues are used by God to achieve His purposes. The protection of the Israelites from the later plagues confirms God is orchestrating the events (Ex. 9:1–6).

The demonstration of power through the plagues declares that Yahweh is God. He alone is worthy of worship and trust. These lessons are not just for the Egyptians, but God is revealing Himself to the Israelites and to Moses. These events transform Moses. Though Moses gets angry with the Israelites after the exodus, after the plagues, he never wavers from his commitment to God or His people.

The revelation of who God is changes us. The Bible shows us we come to know God through life circumstances, including those that devastate. What happens may not be unique, but the timing, the intensity and sequence of events, the context, and the people involved point us to God. If we listen, God will show us who He is in ways that transform and strengthen us. "I will be your God. Then you will know that I am the Lord your God" (Ex. 6:7).

COMPANION THOUGHT

Can you identify a time when you were hit by one disaster after another? How did it affect your view of God then? And now?

YAHWEH VERSUS EGYPTIAN GODS

THE EGYPTIANS WORSHIPPED THOUSANDS OF gods. None of these gods claimed to be all-powerful or exclusive. When Moses asks Pharaoh to let God's people go, Pharaoh asks, "Who is the Lord, that I should obey him?" (Ex. 5:2). The plagues are God's answer. By the time the ten disasters are over, the gods of Egypt are proven powerless, and Pharaoh makes his choices, knowing full well who God is.[75]

<u>Name</u>	<u>Egyptian God</u>	<u>Plague</u>
1. Hapi Osiris, Khnum	Egyptian Gods of the Nile	Water to blood
2. Heqet	Egyptian Goddess of Fertility (head of a frog)	Frogs
3. Geb (Seb)	Egyptian God of the Earth	Lice from dust
4. Khepri Uatchit	Egyptian God of Creation (head of a fly) Egyptian Goddess of Flies	Swarm of flies
5. Amon Hathor, Ptah	King of Egyptian Gods (depicted with ram's head) Egyptian Bull Gods	Death of cattle and livestock
6. Sekhmet Isis, Serapis, Imhotep	Egyptian Goddess of Epidemics Egyptian Gods of Medicine	Boils and sores
7. Nut Seth Shu	Egyptian Goddess of Sky Egyptian God of Agriculture Egyptian God of the Atmosphere	Hail
8. Serapia	Egyptian Protector against Locusts	Locust from skies
9. Ra Aten	Egyptian Sun God	Darkness
10. Pharoah	Egyptian God who assumes power over life and death by killing the Hebrew boys.	Death of Egypt's first- born people and animals

Exodus 9

A HARD HEART

But the Lord hardened Pharaoh's heart, and he would not listen
to Moses and Aaron.

Exodus 9:12

MANY ARE TROUBLED BY THE statement, "The Lord hardened Pharaoh's heart" (Ex. 9:12). If the Lord hardened his heart, how could Pharaoh be responsible for what he did? And if the Lord hardened Pharaoh's heart, does He harden the hearts of other people too? Does this mean there is no personal accountability for our actions?

Scripture notes that with the first seven plagues, Pharaoh hardens his own heart. In the last three plagues, God hardens Pharaoh's heart. God does this through continued revelation. At some point, the truth becomes obvious to Pharaoh—the Hebrew God is not a god, but is *the only* God. This revelation does not break Pharaoh; it infuriates him. Famous preacher Charles Spurgeon observed, "The same sun which melts wax hardens clay. And the same gospel which melts some persons to repentance hardens others in their sins."[76]

The Bible teaches that we are responsible for our choices. God is patient, revealing Himself to us until we have no doubt about who He is and what He asks of us. If we still rebel, then the more we learn about God, the more embittered we can become. Rather than soften us, truth will harden us. The more the Lord reveals Himself, the angrier we can become. "The Lord . . . is patient with you, not wanting anyone to perish, but everyone to come to repentance" (2 Peter 3:9). If we persist in resisting God's truth, He will allow us to continue in the path we have chosen.

COMPANION THOUGHT

Describe a time when you did something, even though you knew it wasn't a good thing to do. Why did you do it?

Exodus 10
NO COMPROMISE

We will go with our young and our old, with our sons and our daughters, and with our flocks and herds.

Exodus 10:9

THE PLAGUES DEVASTATE EGYPT. FOUR times, Pharaoh attempts to negotiate a compromise. The unacceptability of his demands becomes obvious when translated into modern terms:

1. "Go, sacrifice to your God here in the land" (Ex. 8:25). You don't have to make any changes in your life to follow Jesus. Stay where you are (in bondage).
2. "You must not go very far" (Ex. 8:28). Don't burn any bridges. Don't take your religion too far.
3. "Have only the men go" (Ex. 10:11). Don't push religion on your family. Your children can decide for themselves how they want to live when they're older.
4. "Leave your flocks and herds behind" (Ex. 10:24). Keep your possessions and finances separate from your spiritual life.

Standing his ground, Moses gives his final word to Pharaoh: "Not a hoof is to be left behind" (Ex. 10:26).

If Satan cannot stop us from starting a faith journey, he will tempt us to "temper" it by separating our spiritual life from everyday life. He tells us we can serve God without obedience, blinding us to the fact that we are slaves to our schedules, possessions, work, and relationships.

But God asks us to commit all these things to Him. Because He is our Creator, nothing we have belongs solely to us. What we give to the Lord, He will redeem and return to us to freely enjoy. "For whoever wants to save their life will lose it, but whoever loses their life for me will find it" (Matt. 16:25).

COMPANION THOUGHT
If you were Moses, which of the compromises would you have been tempted to make? Why?

Exodus 11
EGYPTIAN GOLD FOR GOD'S TABERNACLE

Tell the people . . . to ask their neighbors for articles of silver and gold.
  Exodus 11:2

MOSES COMMANDS THE RESPECT OF the officials of Pharaoh's court and the Egyptian people (Ex. 7:1). When (at God's instruction) the Hebrews ask their neighbors for articles of gold and silver, the Egyptians generously respond. Perhaps the harsh treatment Pharaoh has inflicted upon the Israelites stirs sympathy. No doubt many Egyptians fear the Hebrews because of the plagues. As predicted, the Israelites "plunder" the Egyptians (Ex. 3:21; 12:36). Soon God will command the Israelites to construct a portable worship center that calls for precious materials far beyond what the slave nation would possess. The wealth of the land that had once enslaved them will beautify God's dwelling place.

In Scripture, Egypt represents the world, sin, and bondage.[77] The redirecting of Egypt's resources for God's glory symbolizes God's power to redeem. Some of the most valued treasures of the church have been gifted by those who have turned from a life of sin to Christ. The converted philosopher Augustine abandoned his immoral life and gave himself to defining the doctrines of faith.[78] John Newton, once a slave trader, became a fervent abolitionist and pastor.[79] The treasures of literature, music, art, business acumen, and technology all have a place in God's kingdom. When God asks us to surrender all to Him, we also surrender the resources and gifts with which we have served the world. What Satan once used to enslave us, God redeems for His glory.

COMPANION THOUGHT
What gift do you have that you would consider "redeemed"?

Exodus 12
THE PASSOVER

The blood will be a sign for you. . . , and when I see the blood, I will pass over you. No destructive plague will touch you when I strike Egypt.
  Exodus 12:13

THE DEATH ANGEL SENT TO kill the Egyptians' firstborn passes over those families who brush the blood of the lamb on their doorposts. To celebrate God's grace, Yahweh establishes Passover as an annual feast (Ex. 12:14–20). As Israel's story unfolds, God will continue to attach symbols and rituals to the Hebrews' encounters with Him. Passover will remind the Israelites that they are not slaves, but are God's children. They belong to the Lord and are now under His protection.

In these early books of the Bible, God systematically reinforces the Israelites' new identity through rituals. The rituals we observe in our time do the same thing—they bind us together and remind us who we are.[80] Though we forget and become distracted, rituals call us back to our roots. They help us remember. "Remembering" in the Bible is more than looking back; it's an intentional reconnecting with the past to encourage us to act in faith today and in the future.[81]

Remembering reinforces identity. God's Word says we are God's children, deeply loved by Him (1 John 3:1). So why is it so hard to believe? Sin and a mistaken view of ourselves get in the way. Romans 6:23 says that our sin condemns us to death and that God's grace is our only hope. John the Baptist introduces Jesus as "the Lamb of God, who takes away the sin of the world" (John 1:29). Accepting Christ's sacrifice for our sins is an act of faith, just as brushing the blood of the lamb on the doorpost was in Moses's day. Faith spares us from death and marks us as God's children. The rituals and disciplines of faith such as prayer, Bible study, communion, the Sabbath, and holy days, remind us of who we are. We belong to God. Our identity and salvation are found in Him.

COMPANION THOUGHT
What meal in your family tradition means the most to you? Why?

Exodus 13

THE BONES OF JOSEPH

Moses took the bones of Joseph with him because Joseph had made the Israelites swear an oath.
    Exodus 13:19

IT HAS BEEN NEARLY FOUR hundred years since Joseph's death, yet as he had requested, the Israelites take Joseph's bones with them as they leave Egypt.

If anyone had reason to love Egypt, it was Joseph. When his brothers had cast him out, Egypt had taken him in. Egypt had given him wealth, fame, and power. His adopted land saved his family from starvation and reunited him with his beloved father and brothers. Despite this, Joseph never considered Egypt his home. He was not an Egyptian—he was an Israelite, a Hebrew. He wanted his final resting place to be in Canaan, the land God promised to Abraham and his descendants. Joseph's request was remembered and honored by the children of Israel. This tells us that the story of God's promise was never lost. Even in Egypt, hope was passed down through the generations.

Vibrant faith won't pass to our descendants unless we are intentional about telling God's story (Deut. 6). Do our children know what the Bible says about who we are? Do they know of times God has rescued us? Our stories are important in our children's faith journeys. Our accounts of God's deliverance, of how He's sustained us and remained faithful to us even when we've failed, are lifelines our children may cling to as they struggle with issues of faith.

COMPANION THOUGHT
What is your favorite family story? When you tell it, how do others react? How could you make spiritual story-telling part of your family tradition?

Exodus 14

CROSSING THE RED SEA

That day the Lord saved Israel from the hands of the Egyptians.
    Exodus 14:30

THE ISRAELITES ARE BARELY OUT of Egypt when they realize Pharaoh's army is pursuing. At the banks of the Red Sea, they turn to see the Egyptian army closing in.

The people panic, but Moses remains calm. Any doubts he had about God's ability to save are gone. The trials of Egypt have proven to him that God can and will protect His people. With boldness, Moses says, "Do not be afraid. Stand firm and you will see the deliverance the Lord will bring you today" (Ex. 14:13).

God parts the waters, and the people walk across the dry bed of the Red Sea. When the Egyptian army follows, the waters rush back in. The Egyptians drown as the Israelites stand safe on the other side. At last, God's people are free.

When we're fighting to survive, we may wonder if freedom is truly possible. Our sins and our circumstances can be so oppressive that we're afraid to hope. The exodus testifies that there is a day of deliverance. God is big and powerful enough to rescue us and work miracles. It's important to note that the freedom God offers does not put us in charge. Our way leads to death (Rom. 6:23). Freedom comes when we acknowledge God's right to rule over us and surrender to Him. The apostle Paul says, "Stand firm, then, and do not let yourselves be burdened again by a yoke of slavery" (Gal. 5:1). Serving God is the path to freedom. "So if the Son sets you free, you will be free indeed" (John 8:36).

COMPANION THOUGHT

Do you feel like: (1) the Israelites, trying to act in faith, but afraid, (2) Moses, confident that God will intervene, or (3) Pharaoh's army, drowning? What could change your perspective?

Exodus 15

THE LORD IS A WARRIOR

The Lord is my strength and my defense; he has become my salvation. . . . The Lord is a warrior.
Exodus 15:2–3

AFTER PHARAOH'S ARMY DROWNS IN the Red Sea, Moses and Miriam lead the Israelites in singing and dancing to celebrate. They offer the first hymn sung in Scripture. In the Bible, a "hymn" is a formal (often poetic) praise to God.[82] The song of Moses and Miriam praises several aspects of God's character:

- **God is a warrior (vv. 2–3).** For the first time, the Israelites stand as a nation and in a spectacular show of strength, God fights for them.[83] God as a warrior will be a major theme in Scripture.
- **God is unlike any other.** "Who among the gods is like you, Lord?" (Ex. 15:11). The parting of the Red Sea demonstrates what God had already proved through the ten plagues—Yahweh is supreme over all gods.
- **God is love.** "In your unfailing love you will lead the people you have redeemed" (v. 13). Abraham's stories, passed down through generations, depicted God as loving and kind (Gen. 24), but a loving God must have been hard for the Hebrews to believe in while enslaved in Egypt. Now they are experiencing God's goodness for themselves.

At some point, what we've heard about God isn't enough. Psalm 34:8 says, "Taste and see that the Lord is good; blessed is the one who takes refuge in him." As we take refuge in God, we find Him good. We may not know much about Him yet, but if we know enough to follow Him, He will rescue us and set us on a path of life.

COMPANION THOUGHT
How do you celebrate life events in your family? Is celebration something you look forward to or dread? Why?

Exodus 16
GRUMBLING

You are not grumbling against us, but against the Lord.
Exodus 16:8

SIX WEEKS LATER, THE STING of the whip has been forgotten. The sound of the Red Sea crashing over the Egyptians has faded from the Israelites' memory. Now they grumble and blame Moses and Aaron for talking them into this journey. They miss Egypt with its bountiful food supply and want to return to the land that had enslaved them. Finally, Moses has had enough. He says, "You are not grumbling against us, but against the Lord" (Ex. 18:8).

Moses is right. If we believe that God is in control of our lives, grumbling is a complaint against God. Grumbling tells God that He's failed to make life what we want it to be. We wonder how the Hebrews could be so ungrateful, having just been delivered from bondage, but if we allow what isn't to our liking to overshadow all that is good in our lives, we are no different.

Grumbling is a sin because it accuses God of doing wrong. It also drags us and others down. Israel's complaining eventually provokes Moses to sin, causing God to deny him entrance into the Promised Land (Num. 20). Despite their complaining, God continues to provide. Each morning, His gift of manna brings a new opportunity to repent and trust.

Trust doesn't come easy if we've been oppressed. Bondage makes us negative and wary. But God is patient. He will allow trying situations to strengthen our faith. We'll know how we're doing by our attitudes. The more we trust God, the more we will recognize His provision and the more grateful we'll become.

COMPANION THOUGHT
What are your "good old days"? What did you like about them? How do they affect your view of today?

AARON

AARON, THE BROTHER OF MOSES, is a significant person in the Bible because of his role in the worship system God establishes. Growing up, Aaron lived as a slave while his younger brother lived as royalty. Yet even though Aaron and Moses lived in different worlds, they bonded as brothers. They share the heritage of Abraham, Isaac, and Jacob and the conviction that God will give His people the land He promised.

When Moses flees after killing a man, Aaron remains in Egypt, sharing in the hardships of the Israelites. Yet God has plans for Aaron too. At the burning bush, God tells Moses that Aaron is on his way to see him (Ex. 4:14, 27). It's the first time Aaron appears in Scripture.

God appoints Aaron as Moses's spokesperson after Moses insists that he (Moses) can't speak well enough to persuade God's people or Pharaoh to listen. Besides being an eloquent speaker, Aaron is a leader in his own right. After Moses's first encounter with Pharaoh ends disastrously, the people want nothing more to do with Moses. But Aaron seems to have used his influence to convince the people to keep listening to his brother. In the end, Exodus 6:26 credits Moses and Aaron with leading the Israelites out of Egypt.

The Scripture's mention of Aaron isn't always positive. Twice, Aaron demonstrates a character weakness. While Moses is hidden at Sinai with the Lord, Aaron yields to the pressure of the people and assists them in making an idol, a golden calf (Ex. 32). Later, he joins his sister Miriam's protest against Moses's authority (Num. 12). Aaron also struggles after his two sons are killed for disrespecting God in the tabernacle.

Overall, Aaron's loyalty to his brother is remarkable. The anger and criticism the Israelites level at Moses during his forty-year leadership also falls on Aaron. When they speak of stoning, Aaron, too, is targeted. During the fight against the Amalekites, Aaron is one of those who holds up Moses's arms, enabling the Israelites to win. Throughout the exodus story, Aaron stands with his brother.

Aaron comes to the forefront in God's instructions regarding the tabernacle. Aaron's line (within the tribe of Levi) is given the privilege of carrying out the rituals of worship and animal sacrifice. God sets apart Aaron and his descendants to mediate between God and the people as priests. Aaron becomes Israel's first high priest (Ex. 29:9).

Because Aaron and Moses are of the tribe of Levi, the religious system that God establishes is known as the Levitical system. This system serves a vital purpose, yet is never intended to be permanent. The sacrificial rituals are symbolic of Jesus's sacrifice for sin on the cross. At Jesus's death, the Levitical system is abolished (Heb. 7:18–19).

Exodus 17

THE POWER OF POSITIVE SUPPORT

Aaron and Hur held his hands up—one on one side, one on the other—so that his hands remained steady.
　　　Exodus 17:12

NO SOONER IS THE ISRAELITES' need for water met than they suffer another threat—an attack by the Amalekites. Moses climbs to the top of a hill where Israel's fighting men can see him, and he holds up his hands to encourage them in battle. "As long as Moses held up his hands, the Israelites were winning, but whenever he lowered his hands, the Amalekites were winning" (Ex. 17:11). When Moses grows tired, Aaron and Hur stand on either side, holding up his hands until the Israelites win.

When in a crisis, support can make the difference between victory and defeat. There are times when we need to be supported and times when we're called to be the support for others. A word of affirmation, a kind gesture, a gift, or a response to a need can lift the spirit of one who is weary.

The Bible reminds us that "a cord of three strands is not quickly broken" (Eccl. 4:12). We are stronger together. The battles we fight on earth are also being waged in the spiritual realm. Both prayer and a helping hand are important to overcoming life's difficulties.

COMPANION THOUGHT

Who typically bears the brunt of your frustration? What kind of support could help you better handle stress?

Exodus 18

TRUE GREATNESS

Moses listened to his father-in-law and did everything he said.
  Exodus 18:24

THOUGH MOSES POSSESSES EXTRAORDINARY TALENTS and abilities, he is wearing down. His father-in-law who cares enough to point it out, counsels Moses to stop doing everything on his own. He also unites Moses with his wife and sons (Ex. 18:5–6). Zipporah and the boys had traveled to Egypt with Moses (Ex. 4:19–26), but at some point, Moses must have sent them back (perhaps to protect them). Not much is said about Moses's family in Scripture. Zipporah is not an Israelite, which could have been difficult for them both, but Moses receives his family and follows Jethro's advice about delegation.

Moses's willingness to listen proves his greatness as a leader. Numbers 12:3 tells us, "Moses was a very humble man, more humble than anyone else on the face of the earth." Slamming into our human limitations reveals our true character. It takes humility to not only acknowledge another person's abilities, but also to relinquish control.

When the Holy Spirit sends someone to correct or question how we do things, how do we respond? Are we defensive, or are we gracious and willing to listen? A humble person recognizes that others have something to offer. If we ask, the Holy Spirit will help us discern what is of value in what we're being told (James 1:5). Moses teaches us that true greatness begins with humility. First Peter 5:5 says, "Clothe yourself with humility toward one another, because, 'God opposes the proud but shows favor to the humble.'"

COMPANION THOUGHT
What was the hardest advice you've ever received? Did you heed it?

Exodus 19

MOSES AT MOUNT SINAI

The Lord descended to the top of Mount Sinai and called Moses to the top of the mountain.
   Exodus 19:20

MOUNT SINAI (ALSO KNOWN AS Mount Horeb) is where God spoke to Moses in the burning bush. Now at this same mountain, God meets with His people. In the weeks to come, He will reaffirm and expand the covenant He made with Abraham and give Israel His Law. Also on this mountain, Moses will meet with God "face to face," a phenomenon so rare that it is noted four times in these early books of the Bible (Ex. 33:11; Num. 14:14; Deut. 5:4; 34:10).

In ancient times, God was perceived as being so far above man that He was unapproachable.[84] Through Moses, God makes it clear that He can be known in a personal way. Until now, God's communication with His people has been intermittent and sparse, but Exodus reveals God can speak through one man who has an intimate relationship with Him. God is laying the groundwork for a seismic change—the God who speaks to Moses face to face is working on a plan to give every person access to the Father. After Jesus's coming, the Holy Spirit will reside within the heart of every believer.

Jesus says, "Anyone who loves me will obey my teaching. My Father will love them, and we will come to them and make our home with them" (John 14:23).

COMPANION THOUGHT

How do you communicate with God? Are you ever afraid to hear God's voice? Why or why not?

Exodus 20

THE TEN COMMANDMENTS

And God spoke all these words.
    Exodus 20:1

EXCITEMENT ELECTRIFIES THE AIR AS the people of Israel push toward the foot of Mount Sinai. After giving a second warning for the people not to rush the mountain, the Lord appears as fire and descends to the mountaintop. The earth quakes. The atmosphere explodes, causing the people to panic. God calls for Moses to join Him on the mountain. Later, God will write the Ten Commandments on stone, but on this day, He speaks the commands to Moses in the hearing of the people (Ex. 19:9, Deut. 4:12-13).

Yahweh's display of power excites the people, but the Law terrifies them. The only ruler the Israelites have known is Pharaoh—a tyrannical, vindictive taskmaster. As they hear the Law, they realize they are not free to do as they wish, but are exchanging one master for another. The first law, *no other gods*, hits hard. Israel knows little about Yahweh. Why should they trust Him? What if He is worse than Pharaoh? What if they can't keep the Law or don't want to obey? Afraid, the people distance themselves and ask that God only speak to them through Moses (Ex. 20:18–21). Fear keeps them from seeing the Law as God's gift.

The Bible shows us how obeying God's law brings life. Over the centuries, religious leaders complicate the Law with human interpretations. Jesus, however, does the opposite. He distills the Law into two commands: (1) "Love the Lord your God with all your heart and with all your soul and with all your mind," and (2) "Love your neighbor as yourself" (Matt. 22:37–40).

A paradox of faith is that we are free only when we submit ourselves to God's authority. His laws aren't meant to repress, but to keep us from destroying ourselves (Rom. 7). "But now that you have been set free from sin and have become slaves of God, the benefit you reap leads to holiness, and the result is eternal life" (Rom. 6:22).

COMPANION THOUGHT

Who sets the rules in your house? What effect do the rules have on your household—do they make things better or worse? Why?

THE TEN COMMANDMENTS

Exodus 20:2–17

1. You shall have no other gods before me.
2. You shall not make for yourself an idol.
3. You shall not misuse the name of the Lord your God.
4. Observe the Sabbath day by keeping it holy.
5. Honor your father and mother.
6. You shall not murder.
7. You shall not commit adultery.
8. You shall not steal.
9. You shall not give false testimony against your neighbor.
10. You shall not covet.

Exodus 21
AN EYE FOR AN EYE

If there is serious injury, you are to take life for life, eye for eye, tooth for tooth, hand for hand.
Exodus 21:23–24

AFTER GIVING THE PRINCIPLES OF the Law, God applies the Law to real-life situations.[85] These applications are essentially "case law"—examples meant to guide future legal decisions.[86] God is fleshing out a new covenant with His people. The Abrahamic covenant gave the Israelites the land of Canaan and promised a posterity that would bless the earth (through the Messiah and His "family" of believers).[87] The Mosaic covenant is detailed and focuses on how God's people are to live.

The Old Testament law of "an eye for an eye" is often misunderstood. It is sometimes called *the law of retaliation*, but the purpose of this law is not to justify vengeance, but to limit punishment so that it fits the crime.[88]

In the Sermon on the Mount, Jesus takes this law further, saying that the offended person is obligated to do more than show restraint—they should diligently seek to do good to the offender (Matt. 5:38). We are to love all people, including those who have hurt us, and we are to express that love in positive deeds. The Law seeks justice and endeavors to bring appropriate punishment to the offender. Grace, on the other hand, embraces the goal of forgiveness and seeks to restore the relationship.

Jesus teaches us to take the high road of grace and forgiveness. There may be a place for judgment and punishment in the civil legal system, but not in the arena of our personal relationships. The law of love transcends the legal position of "an eye for an eye."

COMPANION THOUGHT
In your house as you were growing up, did the punishment fit the crime? How does your experience affect how discipline is carried out in your home today?

HOW TO READ THE LAW

IN SCRIPTURE, *THE LAW* REFERS to the commandments, judgments, codes, and ordinances given to Moses.[89] These laws recorded in the books of Exodus, Leviticus, Numbers, and Deuteronomy apply the Ten Commandments, teaching us how to relate to God and our fellow human beings.[90]

The goriness of animal sacrifice and the repetition of tedious legal statutes makes the books of the Law a tough read. Yet these passages are also the inspired Word of God, and as such, we are compelled to search out their meanings.

The treasure in these passages can only be appreciated through the lens of the New Testament. New Testament writers tell us that the primary purpose of the Law is to reveal sin (Rom. 7:7–25). Today the Holy Spirit convicts of sin (John 16:8), but the Law still guides us. The Law and its rituals are also heavy with symbolism that makes the enormity of Jesus's sacrifice clear to us. Believing Jews in the New Testament show us how Jesus is the fulfillment of Levitical law.

As we seek to understand how the Law applies to us today, several perspectives give us insight.

THE GENRE OF THE LAW

Genre is a term that means "a particular type of category of literature or art."[91] We read books differently depending on their type (e.g., history, poetry, fiction).[92] We don't approach a novel the same way we would an auto repair manual. In biblical times, the Law was seen as an instruction book within God's story, consisting of two parts: sacrifices and moral codes.

1. **Sacrifices.** The instructions about offerings and sacrifices are directed toward the priests. The details are like recipes that call for prescribed ingredients to be prepared in a specific way. As readers, we should avoid getting lost in the details, and instead focus on the bigger picture. What is the purpose of the sacrifice? What about each sacrifice applies to us today?
2. **Moral code.** The second half of the Law applies to the lay person (those who are not priests). These laws set the purity standards for individuals and society. If God is to dwell among them, the Israelites must live as a holy people; however, the priests will be expected to model and teach these laws to the community and to hold the people accountable.

There's no denying that the books of the Law lack the devotional quality found in the poetic books such as Psalms and Proverbs. If we find ourselves longing for more of an emotional connection to Scripture than we're getting from the legal passages, consider reading a psalm along with the Law. One often sheds light on the other.

THE PASSING AND THE PERMANENT[93]

Christ's death does away with the need for ongoing sacrifices. Jesus frees us from onerous rule-keeping that is part of the Levitical system, but the principles underlying the Law remain:[94]

- Respect for the holiness of God.

- Our need for atonement.
- The call to morality.
- The mandate to create a just society that reflects the dignity God imparts to all living things.

Identifying what is *passing* and what is *permanent* will help us sort out which ancient laws apply to us today.

SEED TRUTHS

The Law does not speak directly to every social ill that has or will afflict mankind, but the perspective of *seed truths* helps us identify God's intent, even if it's not overtly stated. In Scripture, God doesn't always confront thorny issues immediately, but brings about greater revelation in the fullness of time (Gal. 4:4).[95] Little by little, the Holy Spirit brings an understanding of truth that was there all along. But Scripture was written in a particular time and place, and the context of that time period must guide us as we deal with assumptions in the Law that we find unsettling. The laws regarding slaves and women are two examples.

Exodus 21:20 refers to a slave as property. This perspective acknowledges life as it was at the time and should not be taken as approval of slavery. God's law limits the power of the oppressor until deliverance comes. The *seed truth* principle recognizes that God's intent is liberty for all. This is the thrust of the gospel from beginning to end. Long before slavery is outlawed, the gospel abolishes the prejudices, hate, and greed that make slavery possible.

Regarding women, Genesis tells us that all men and women are made in God's image (Gen. 1:26–28, 5:1–3; 9:6). In the New Testament, Paul says, "There is neither Jew nor Gentile, neither slave nor free, nor is there male and female, for you are all one in Christ Jesus" (Gal. 3:28).

The cross has overcome all racial, social, political, and religious divisions (Eph. 2:11–22). The gospel teaches us how to navigate the realities of our fallen world, even as it plants seeds of God's truth that will ultimately displace all evil.

HOLINESS

The Law teaches the Israelites how to distinguish between what is clean and unclean, holy and unholy. Though the sacrificial system is no longer the means of relating to God, God's truth can still be seen in the symbols of worship and the practicality of the Law's civil codes. Today, reading the Law reminds us that God requires those who are called by His name to live holy lives—yet we quickly realize that the Law is impossible to keep! It makes sense that as we work through the complicated rituals of worship, sacrifice, and daily life—we feel the weight of the Law. That is the point. The Law, from the beginning, is burdensome and insufficient (Heb. 10). We need a Savior. Keeping this in mind focuses our attention where it belongs—on the grace of God. We can be grateful to the Law for teaching us how much we need salvation, but we have no reason to fear it. The Law informs us, but does not bind us.

Exodus 22
RESTITUTION

Anyone who steals must certainly make restitution.
Exodus 22:3

PERSONAL RESPONSIBILITY, A RECURRING PRINCIPLE in Scripture, is based on Mosaic law. The Law demands we make restitution if our actions cause bodily harm or loss of property to another person. Jesus takes this further, teaching that when we've given another person cause for offense, we must go to the offended person and make things right (Matt. 5:23–24).

Exodus chapter 22 details various situations in which restitution is required. Many of the laws stated in Exodus have become the basis for our current legal system. They include everything from accidental loss to deliberate violent acts. Protection for the vulnerable—women, the poor, the slave—is a defining characteristic of Mosaic law. The insistence of both justice and restraint sets a moral standard unequaled in Moses's time.

While other Near Eastern cultures had written legal codes with parts similar to the Mosaic law, God's Law is unique in its spiritual emphasis.[96] It addresses the cause of transgression, not just the result of the offense. The law of Moses frames sin against others as sin against God and gives great value to life. Mosaic law sets the holiness of God as the standard of behavior for individuals and society. Finally, the sacrificial system described in Leviticus reveals that relationship is God's top priority. Unlike other codes, God's law offers a way of forgiveness. The means of animal sacrifices cannot atone for sin and is temporary, yet it demonstrates faith in God's promise of providing atonement. Those who lived before Jesus came were saved just as we are—by believing God. They looked toward the cross, and we look back to the cross. But the blood of Jesus covers the sins of all who trust in Him. " For it is by grace you have been saved, through faith—and this is not from yourselves, it is the gift of God" (Eph. 2:8).

COMPANION THOUGHT

Do your community's policies toward abused children or women, immigrants, the poor, or disabled reflect God's heart for the vulnerable? How or how not?

Exodus 23

WELCOMING STRANGERS

Do not oppress a foreigner; you yourselves know how it feels to be foreigners, because you were foreigners in Egypt.
        Exodus 23:9

THE KING JAMES TRANSLATES *"ALIENS"* or *"foreigners"* as *"strangers."* The word refers to people living in our midst who are not like us. Exodus 12:38 (NKJV) speaks of a "mixed multitude" who joined Israel's exodus from Egypt. Egyptians and those from other nations who believed in God's promise were to be welcomed. In ancient times, most nations dealt harshly with foreigners. By contrast, the Hebrews are instructed to show special kindness and consideration to them. The Mosaic law forbids God's people to oppress strangers or to make life more difficult for them.[97]

Throughout the Old Testament, God reminds the Israelites that they were once aliens in Egypt. Knowing how it feels to be mistreated, the Hebrews are to be sensitive to displaced people. A willingness to welcome outsiders and give special consideration to those of other nationalities will become a distinctive of Judeo-Christian culture. In God's kingdom, there are to be no second-class citizens.

Showing kindness to the stranger, a tenant woven into the fabric of Israel's legal system, should guide our treatment of those who are different from us. The principle applies not only to those from other countries, but also to those who are not of our ethnic, economic, social, or political group. We tend to gravitate toward "our kind of people." As Christians who once were alienated from Christ and are now part of God's family, we have a responsibility to show kindness to any person or people group that is marginalized.

COMPANION THOUGHT
Describe a time you were mistreated because you were different. How did you feel? How has this experience influenced how you treat outsiders?

Exodus 24
MOSES, THE MEDIATOR OF GOD'S COVENANT

Moses alone is to approach the Lord; the others must not come near.
Exodus 24:2

THE ISRAELITES QUICKLY ASSENT TO the terms of the covenant and seal it through a blood ritual (the blood, sprinkled on the people and the altar, binds both God and the people). God then invites Moses, Aaron, Aaron's two sons, and seventy of Israel's leaders to a celebration feast (Ex. 24:9). They see God (perhaps Jesus, God in human form),[98] and afterward, God calls Moses to meet Him on the mountain. In Near Eastern treaties, each party was to receive a copy of the covenant.[99] The tablets God intends to give Moses will fulfill this last requirement (v. 12).

Moses has a unique place in Old Testament history and theology. He alone is chosen to mediate the covenant between God and the people of Israel. For the next fifteen hundred years, Moses will occupy a place of authority and honor in Jewish history unequaled by any other person. However, ultimately Moses is superseded by Jesus (Heb. 3 :1–6). While Moses is the mediator of the old covenant of the Law, Jesus is the mediator of the new covenant of grace (Heb. 12:24). Jesus is the full and final revelation of God to man (Col. 2:9).

Yet Jesus says, "Do not think that I have come to abolish the Law or the Prophets; I have not come to abolish them but to fulfill them" (Matt. 5:17). The Law remains important in establishing the foundations of Christian belief and practice:

- The Law is an expression of God's holiness (Rom. 3:23–24).
- The Law convicts of sin (Rom. 3:19–20).
- The Law points to Jesus, calling for faith as the basis for forgiveness (Gal. 3:24).
- Our obedience to the Law witnesses to the world that we belong to Christ (Rom. 3:31).

COMPANION THOUGHT
Have you ever had an encounter with someone that changed your life? Who was it? How did the experience change you?

Exodus 25
THE TABERNACLE

Make this tabernacle and all its furnishings exactly like the pattern I will show you.
Exodus 25:9

THE TABERNACLE HAS AN IMMEDIATE and future use. As a temporary portable structure, it serves as a sanctuary—the place God agrees to meet with His people. But it also foreshadows the new covenant God intends to make with creation.

The long-term purpose of the tabernacle becomes clear after Jesus comes. The New Testament teaches that the floor plan, the furnishings, the materials used, and the colors of the materials of the tabernacle all symbolize specifics aspects of Christ and His redemptive work. That is why God insists Moses make everything exactly according to His instructions. God repeats this injunction in four different passages (Ex. 25:9, 40; Ex. 26:30; Num. 8:4). Although the plan sounds restrictive, the structure offers freedom. God Himself will commission certain people to design the tabernacle. Inspired by the Holy Spirit, these artisans will put their own stamp on the work (Ex. 31:2–6).

God lays the pattern for our salvation and arranges and beautifies what goes into our journey. He knows what is best for us and how what we experience today will prepare us for tomorrow. It is not for us to determine our own course without considering God's priorities, and we are not free to adjust our beliefs according to what we think. Our place is to follow the plan God gives us in His Word. Obedience brings freedom and inspiration. God's pattern suits His purpose and gives us our best chance for fulfillment and peace. "You shall walk in all the ways which the Lord your God has commanded you, that you may live and that it may be well with you" (Deut. 5:33 NKJV).

COMPANION THOUGHT
Have you ever created a disaster by not following a recipe or instructions as given? What happened?

THE TABERNACLE AND ITS FURNISHINGS

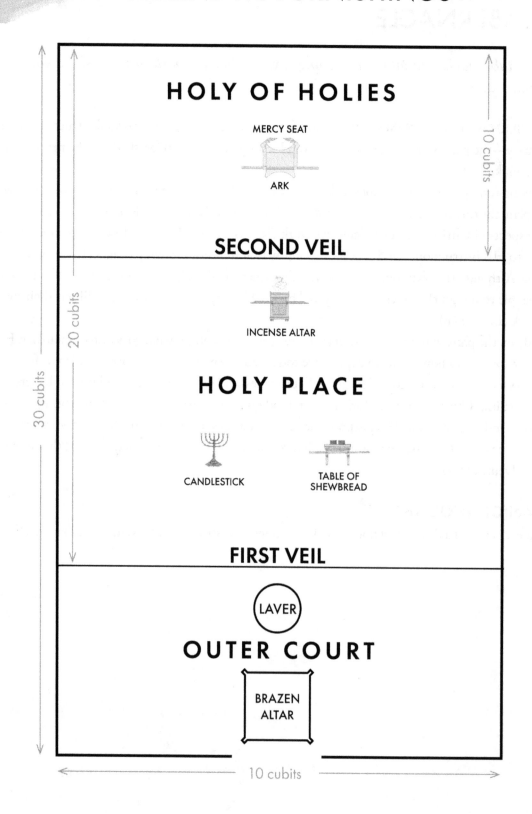

Exodus 26
AN IMPORTANT CURTAIN

Make a curtain of blue, purple and scarlet yarn and finely twisted linen. . . . The curtain will separate the Holy Place from the Most Holy Place.
　　Exodus 26:31, 33

INSIDE THE TABERNACLE IS AN enclosed rectangular space called "the Holy Place." Behind it, separated by a thick curtain (the inner veil), is a small cubicle, fifteen feet long by fifteen feet high, called the Most Holy Place or the Holy of Holies (Ex. 26:31–33). No one is permitted to enter this sacred space except for the high priest, and he only once a year on the Day of Atonement (Ex. 30:10). The curtain prevents anyone who is not authorized from entering. Years later, the permanent temple that replaces the wilderness tabernacle will follow the same pattern: a veil will separate the Most Holy Place from the place of sacrifice and worship.

The New Testament records an amazing event at Jesus's death. The moment that Jesus gives up His spirit, "the curtain of the temple was torn in two from top to bottom" (Matt. 27:51). The wall separating us from God is literally and symbolically abolished, giving each of us full access to God's presence. Soon after Jesus ascends into heaven, the Holy Spirit falls on believers and forever changes how we experience God. Not only is God now with us, but He is also in us. Paul asks, "Do you not realize that Christ Jesus is in you?" (2 Cor. 13:5). Too often, the answer is "no." If we are living without hope, depressed about our circumstances and our world, we've forgotten that God has made His home in our hearts (Eph. 3:17). The love, power, and resources we need to live as our Heavenly Father has commanded are ours for the asking.

COMPANION THOUGHT
Think of a time you were separated from someone you loved for a long time. What was it like when you finally got together?

Exodus 27
THE HORNS OF THE ALTAR

Make a horn at each of the four corners, so that the horns and the altar are of one piece.
Exodus 27:2

THE PHRASE "THE HORNS OF the altar," is first found in God's instructions for building the altar of burnt offering. The horns project from the four corner posts of the altar. When sacrifices are made, some of the blood of the slain animal is to be placed on the horns (Ex. 29:12).

In ancient cultures, the "horn" symbolized strength, honor, fierceness, power, and even royalty.[100] In the Bible, a person in jeopardy could seek God's protection by clinging to the horns of the altar. (In 1 Kings 1:50 and 2:28, Adonijah and Joab run to the altar to avoid being killed by Solomon). Today, "holding to the horns of the altar" has come to mean "standing in persistent and unrelenting prayer" or "to throw ourselves on the mercy of God."[101]

When in trouble, the idea of holding to the horns of the altar can be assuring. The horns in the Holy of Holies remind us that God's atoning work is powerful. Jesus's sacrifice not only cleanses, but protects. No one can touch us when we hold to the Lord. We cannot save ourselves, but God, whose strength is represented by the horns of the altar, can. "The Lord is my rock, my fortress and my deliverer; my God is my rock, in whom I take refuge, my shield and the horn of my salvation, my stronghold" (Ps. 18:2).

COMPANION THOUGHT

Where is your "safe place"? Who is allowed in? How can a sanctuary be a place from which you take on the world?

Exodus 28

THE PRIESTHOOD

Make garments for Aaron, for his consecration, so he may serve me as priest.
   Exodus 28:3

GOD DESIGNS THE RELIGIOUS SYSTEM of the Mosaic law to be administered by a special category of people He designates as priests. Priests are to be mediators who represent the people to God and appeal to God on their behalf. The first high priest is Aaron, the brother of Moses (Ex. 30:10). Aaron and his descendants will serve God and the people through precise rituals that we will read about in Leviticus.

As with the construction of the tabernacle, the details of the priestly garments have symbolic meaning. The high priest will carry the names of the sons of Israel on his shoulders and on his breastplate. Neither Moses nor Aaron, nor any of the high priests who follow him, will understand the full implications of this gesture. One day, Jesus, the Messiah, who from the moment of creation has carried us close to His heart, will bear the weight of our sin on His shoulders.

Jesus, our great high priest, is the mediator between God and man. He tells us to come boldly into God's throne of grace (Heb. 4:14–16). As believers with direct access to God, we share in Christ's priestly role. It's our privilege and calling to bring our loved ones, and those who are in need in our world, before God's throne. We stand in for them, perhaps calling them by name. We hold them near our hearts, care for them, and love them. We intercede as the Holy Spirit guides, offering prayers they may not yet be able to pray for themselves. What Christ, our great high priest, has done for us, we now do in measure for others.

COMPANION THOUGHT
Do you dress differently at home than for work, sports, a wedding, a funeral, or worship? Why?

Exodus 29

PREPARATION FOR LIVING IN GOD'S PRESENCE

They will know that I am the Lord their God, who brought them out of Egypt so that I might dwell among them.
Exodus 29:46

THE PRIESTS MUST UNDERGO EXTENSIVE preparation for their sacred duties. Their outward preparation symbolizes the inward consecration God requires of His people if He is to live among them. Up until now in Scripture, we have seen God visit the patriarchs and prophets, but we have not seen Him living among humankind. God has always wanted to dwell with us. For this to happen, we must become holy. "[God] chose us in him before the creation of the world to be holy and blameless in his sight" (Eph. 1:4).

The overwhelming instructions in Exodus chapters 25–31 remind us how difficult and impossible the task of becoming *holy* is. We will never be able to "clean ourselves up." For a human to become holy takes the supernatural work of God. The Old Testament proves the inadequacy of our best efforts (Heb. 10:1–4), but anticipating Jesus, God grants grace to a human high priest to forgive sins. Through a symbolic animal sacrifice, the high priest can make atonement for the people once a year. It's not obedience to the Law that saves the Israelites, but the faith it takes for them to obey. Even in the Old Testament, faith, not works, is the basis for salvation.

The priests' exhaustive preparation rituals demonstrate how great a gap exists between God and human beings. Our job, as God's ministers, is to share the good news that Jesus has bridged that gap.[102] But before we can help others, we must receive God's grace ourselves. "God's law was given so that all people could see how sinful they were. But as people sinned more and more, God's wonderful grace became more abundant. So just as sin ruled over all people and brought them to death, now God's wonderful grace rules instead, giving us right standing with God and resulting in eternal life through Jesus Christ our Lord" (Rom. 5:20–21 NLT).

COMPANION THOUGHT

Have you ever been to an ordination or consecration service? What do you think is the purpose of such rituals? Are they for God's benefit or for ours?

Exodus 30
THE ANOINTING OIL

Anoint Aaron and his sons . . . so they may serve me as priests.
Exodus 30:30

PART OF THE CONSECRATION OF Aaron and his sons includes a ceremonial anointing. God gives instructions for the oil to be made of a particular blend of oils and spices. The oil's fragrance imprints the moment of consecration into the hearts and memories of the anointed and those who witness it. Anointing with this sacred oil declares that the priestly work of Aaron and his sons is not of human design, but is divinely ordained.

From ancient times, anointing with oil has been a ritual that seeks or affirms God's blessing on a person, usually in the context of commissioning. (The prophet Samuel anoints Saul and later David to be kings of Israel [1 Sam. 10:1; 16:13].)

Anointing oil invites God to mark and empower the one set aside for God's service. For the person receiving the anointing, the ritual is one of submission, acknowledging dependence on God to accomplish the given task. In Scripture, oil is a symbol of the Holy Spirit that leaves a sweet aroma wherever it is used. John writes to believers, "You have an anointing from the Holy One" (1 John 2:20). Paul says, "[God] anointed us . . . and put his Spirit in our hearts" (2 Cor. 1:21–22).

God's anointing is available for each believer. We've been commissioned to the priestly work of making Christ known to our family, our friends, and our world, a task we can only fulfill through the power of the Holy Spirit. "But you will receive power when the Holy Spirit comes on you; and you will be my witnesses in Jerusalem, in all Judea and Samaria, and to the ends of the earth" (Acts 1:8).

COMPANION THOUGHT
What is your favorite smell? Does it make you think of certain people, places, or moments? What do you taste, hear, and feel when a smell triggers that memory?

Exodus 31

THE SABBATH

Say to the Israelites, "You must observe my Sabbaths. This will be a sign between me and you for the generations to come."

Exodus 31:13

THE SABBATH—THE SEVENTH DAY—IS FIRST mentioned in Genesis where God "sanctifies" His creative work by resting. But the command to observe the Sabbath as a holy day does not appear in Scripture until it's given as the fourth commandment: "Remember the Sabbath day by keeping it holy" (Ex. 20:8).

Exodus chapter 31 presents the Sabbath not only as holy, but as a sign of the covenant between God and Israel. With the coming of Christ, we are no longer obligated to the Sabbath as a ritual. We do, however, have compelling scriptural reasons for observing the Sabbath principle: (1) God's example at creation; (2) Sabbath rest is included as one of the Ten Commandments; and (3) the Sabbath's impact on a person and society.

Jesus says, "The Sabbath was made for man, not man for the Sabbath" (Mark 2:27). The Sabbath sanctifies our lives and work as we affirm the following:[103]

- We are more than beasts of burden—we are God's beloved.
- We are more than a body—we have a soul that is to be nourished too.
- We are meant to be free—only the free have the option of rest.
- We are all meant to partake of God's goodness—the call to rest is for everyone.
- We are to make space for unhurried time to God, family, and the community.
- We are stewards, obligated to provide rest to all of God's creation, including animals and the land.

COMPANION THOUGHT

What makes you feel like a beast of burden? What restores your spirit?

Exodus 32

THE GOLDEN CALF

They gave me the gold, and I threw it into the fire, and out came this calf!
     Exodus 32:24

THE GOLDEN CALF INCIDENT HAPPENS soon after Israel's deliverance. For forty days, the Israelites wait in the desert for Moses. The Hebrews have seen Yahweh defeat the gods of Egypt. They've experienced miraculous deliverance from slavery. They've pledged exclusive loyalty to the God of Abraham, Isaac, and Jacob. Yet without a strong leader, the nervous nation defaults to its pagan practices. The Israelites trade off the invisible God for an object that is powerless, but tangible.

Rather than encourage the people to remain faithful, Aaron directs their making of a golden calf. After building an altar, he announces, "Tomorrow there will be a festival to the Lord" (Ex. 32:5). Aaron tries to have it both ways. He gives the people an idol, and he offers sacrifices to Yahweh. This mixing of holy and profane worship deepens Aaron's betrayal.

When Moses descends from the mountain and sees the golden calf, he throws down the tablets of stone on which God had written the Law (v. 19). Moses will have reason to regret this later, but in the heat of the moment, he sees only that the people have broken the covenant. The broken tablets reflect the state of the Israelites' relationship with God. Because of sin, something sacred is lost and there are grave consequences for all. Many Israelites die that day. The future of the Israelites hangs in the balance as God decides what He will do (Ex. 33:5).

We are most likely to falter when we feel abandoned. Times of intense aloneness come to us all, but being aware that we're vulnerable helps us take steps to protect ourselves. We all have certain situations (or people) that tempt us. Choose them, and we fall. Turn to God's Word and to those who support our faith, and we will stand. "Blessed is the one who perseveres under trial because, having stood the test, that person will receive the crown of life that the Lord has promised to those who love him" (James 1:12).

COMPANION THOUGHT

Think of a time when you felt that God was silent. How did it affect your faith?

Exodus 33

A LONGING TO SEE GOD'S GLORY

Then Moses said, "Now show me your glory."
    Exodus 33:18

THOUGH "THE LORD WOULD SPEAK to Moses face to face, as one speaks to a friend" (Ex. 33:11), Moses pushes the limits of their relationship to intercede for the people. Moses has just experienced a brutal disappointment. His brother (the one person he thought he could trust) and the people have forsaken Yahweh. Yet Moses balks when God says He will give the Israelites the land but won't go with them (v. 3). The humble leader reminds God that Yahweh's reputation is on the line. Though God finally agrees to continue to journey with them (vv. 12–14), Moses presses: "If your Presence does not go with us, do not send us up from here" (v. 15). As a sign that God will not relent, Moses asks to see God's face. God denies him, saying, "You cannot see my face, for no one may see me and live" (v. 20);[104] however, God will allow Moses to watch His glory pass by.

There are dimensions of God that will remain beyond human understanding or experience, but there is much of God we can know. Moses says to God, "If you are pleased with me, teach me your ways so I may know you" (v. 13). If we offer that same prayer, God will answer us as he did Moses: "I will do the very thing you have asked, because I am pleased with you and I know you by name" (v. 17). A prayer to know God intimately is one God always answers. We may not get the specific thing we want from Him, but what God does give—His presence, mercy, and compassion—will sustain us through the disappointments and hardships of our journey.

COMPANION THOUGHT

Do you feel as if God knows you by name? Do you think He likes you? How do you think He sees you?

Exodus 34

THE GLOW OF GOD'S PRESENCE

He was not aware that his face was radiant.
      Exodus 34:29

GOD CALLS MOSES BACK TO the mountain and tells him to chisel out two stones like those Moses had broken (Ex. 32:3). The first time, God provided the stones (Ex. 31:18). Now Moses must not only make the tablets, but he must also carry them up the mountain (Ex. 34:1-4). The Ten Commandments had been carved into the stones by the finger of God—they were sacred. Moses had no right to break the tablets, but anger got the best of him. Anger will be a life issue for Moses, but on this day, everyone gets a new start. Once again, God writes the terms of the Covenant on tablets of stone and then allows Moses to see His glory. As God passes by, He declares who He is.

Knowing who God is settles many of our questions and fears. God says He is "the Lord, the Lord, the compassionate and gracious God, slow to anger, abounding in love and faithfulness, maintaining love to thousands, and forgiving wickedness, rebellion and sin" (Ex. 34:6–7). After forty days, Moses goes down the mountain confident that God will go with the Israelites. His face glows from the time he has spent in God's presence. The radiance is so bright that Moses must cover his face to keep from blinding others.

As we grow in our walk with the Lord, our lives take on qualities that others notice: "love, joy, peace, forbearance, kindness, goodness, faithfulness, gentleness and self control" (Gal. 5:22–23). This fruit of the Holy Spirit is evidence of God in our lives. When we stay close to the Lord, He shines through us. We may not be aware of it, but as we reflect God's light, others see that God is present and active in our lives.

COMPANION THOUGHT
What have you done out of anger that you regretted? Were you able to make it right? If so, how?

Exodus 35

LOVE GIFTS FOR GOD'S TABERNACLE

Everyone who is willing is to bring to the Lord an offering.
  Exodus 35:5

AS SLAVES, THE HEBREWS ENRICHED Egypt's coffers against their wills. But now, God's children can choose whether to give their time and treasure to Yahweh. It's not a coincidence that the opportunity to give follows the commandment of observing the Sabbath as a day of rest. Slaves don't rest. Slaves have no choices. God's invitation for His people to partner with Him in creating a sacred place for worship makes a bold statement—God's children are no longer slaves. They are free. The tabernacle will require materials, as well as the skills of craftsmen and artisans, but there is no compulsion. The construction of God's dwelling place is to be a work of love. Rather than tax each family, a call goes out for voluntary contributions. The response is impressive:

Everyone who was *willing*, and whose heart moved him, came and brought an offering to the Lord (v. 21).
All who were *willing*, men and women alike, came and brought gold jewelry of all kinds (v. 22).
All the women who were *willing* and had the skill spun the goat hair (v. 26).
All the Israelite men and women who were *willing* brought to the Lord freewill offerings (v. 29).

Are we quick to respond when God makes us aware of a need? What does it say about us if we're not? It is not usually lack of resources that stops us, but rather a fear that there won't be enough left to meet our needs. If we live as slaves, our mindset will be one of scarcity. If we live as free children of God, we will trust God's abundance. God lavishes us with gifts and resources to use for His glory. He invites us to partner with Him in building His kingdom, but He won't force us. "God loves a cheerful giver" (2 Cor. 9:7).

COMPANION THOUGHT
Do you consider giving an obligation or a privilege? Why?

Exodus 36

MORE THAN ENOUGH

The people were restrained from bringing more, because what they already had was more than enough.
    Exodus 36:6–7

GOD HAD ASKED THE ISRAELITES to bring freewill offerings to pay for the tabernacle (Ex. 35:4–9). The goods and services people bring exceed what is needed to build the sacred space (Ex. 36:4). The Israelites' gifts express more than the generosity of people; they speak of God's abundance. How else could this poverty-stricken people, so recently released from slavery, possess enough wealth to fund a magnificent worship center in the middle of the desert? The tabernacle witnesses of God's ability to reverse fortunes and do the impossible. God has given His people Egypt's treasures (Ex. 3:19–22), and in gratitude, they give to Yahweh's exquisite house of worship.

When we are in bondage, scarcity dominates our lives. We live in fear that there will not be enough. In Christ, we are free to serve because our resources are unlimited. The Bible does not teach a prosperity gospel where we "give to get." God looks at our hearts (1 Sam. 16:7). Our motivation for giving is to be gratitude, not greed. Do we seek blessings for ourselves, or do we look for opportunities to share what God has already given us with others?

Giving does not deplete us; it renews us spiritually and often materially. With God, there is always enough. "And God is able to bless you abundantly, so that in all things at all times, having all that you need, you will abound in every good work" (2 Cor. 9:8).

COMPANION THOUGHT
If someone gave you ten million dollars, what would you do with it?

Exodus 37

A TASK OF HONOR

Bezalel made the ark of acacia wood.
    Exodus 37:1

THE TABERNACLE IS A WORK of art. During their slavery, Israel's craftsmen had been conscripted to build Egyptian temples and palaces. No longer. Now, with willing hands, artisans will make furnishings for the house of God. God selects Bezalel and gives him special skills beyond those he already possesses for this purpose. "Then the Lord said to Moses, 'See, I have chosen Bezalel . . . , and I have filled him with the Spirit of God, with wisdom, with understanding, with knowledge and with all kinds of skills— to make artistic designs'" (Ex. 31:1-4).

Bezalel is given the honor of making the most sacred item in the tabernacle—the ark of the covenant. The ark is the only item of furnishing in the Most Holy Place. Precise instructions are given for its construction. Reflecting God's high worth, the materials for the ark are the finest, most valuable, and purest available. The tabernacle is portable so it can be carried with God's people as they journey to the Promised Land. God does not "live" in the box, but the ark becomes the symbol of God's presence.

The skills, abilities, and passions God gives us are meant first to glorify Him and then to witness of God's presence in us and through us. "Each of you should use whatever gift you have received to serve others, as faithful stewards of God's grace in its various forms" (1 Peter 4:10). Our gifts create beauty meant to bless the church and our world.

COMPANION THOUGHT
Do you think church buildings should be extravagant or humble? Why?

Exodus 38

FURNISHING FOR THE TABERNACLE AND THE COURTYARD

Next they made the courtyard.
    Exodus 38:9

IN CUBITS, THE OUTER COURT of the tabernacle measures 100 x 50 x 5. In feet, this dimension translates to 150 x 75 x 7½ feet high, or around 450 square feet. Though small, the identity, life, and culture of the Jewish nation will form around this sacred space. Each detail of the tabernacle has symbolic meaning.

It will fall to the priests (the Levites) to teach the people the significance of these symbols, but the concept is simple: *God is holy, and we cannot approach Him without being purified.* The tabernacle and all that is inside reinforces this truth. Everything pertaining to God is made of gold. The furnishings outside the most holy spaces relating to sacrifice and cleansing are made of lesser materials. A series of wood posts and rods holding panels of pure linen form the outer courtyard. The white linen's dramatic visual effect is deliberate, announcing that one must be clean to enter.

Today these details feel tedious, but at the time, the Levitical system does the following:

- Temporarily provides forgiveness for sins so that God can dwell among His people.
- Provides rituals of worship that remind the people of who God is and what He's done.
- Reinforces identity with rituals that bind the people to God and each other.
- Foreshadows Jesus. The symbolism of the sacrificial system will reveal the significance of Jesus's sacrifice to future generations.

Today, sacred spaces still call us to faith. They remind us that God is holy, that He has made a way for us to be in relationship to Him, that we are part of His family, and that we have a mission to proclaim Jesus to the generations that follow us.

COMPANION THOUGHT

What is the most stunning building you have ever been in? What about it captured your attention? How did it make you feel? How does it compare to how you feel in your church?

Exodus 39

THE TABERNACLE IS COMPLETED

So all the work on the tabernacle, the tent of meeting, was completed. . . . Moses inspected the work and saw that they had done it just as the Lord had commanded. So Moses blessed them.
Exodus 39:32, 43

ALL OF THE RITUALS OF worship, including sacrifices, will be carried out in the tabernacle. Animal sacrifices were well understood in ancient Near Eastern cultures and were part of Israel's religious practice. Until now, Hebrew sacrifices had been made on open altars without any set form or order. They were sporadic. The new Levitical system makes worship the center of daily life. Moses's blessing of the people—an acknowledgment of their obedience—is a sweet moment for the Israelites.

What sets God's system apart from the religious practices of surrounding nations is its purpose. Other religions called for sacrifices to appease the gods. The Levitical law requires sacrifices for forgiveness of sins. Pagan religions offered no forgiveness because relationship with their gods was not possible.[105] But atonement is essential to Yahweh, who desires to live with His people.

Only through forgiveness of sins can we be made holy. Later God explains, "On this day atonement will be made for you, to cleanse you. Then, before the Lord, you will be clean from all your sins" (Lev. 16:30). Before the first atoning sacrifice, God met with Moses and the leaders in the "tent of meeting" outside the camp (Ex. 33:7). After the sacrifice, God moves inside the camp, to the sanctuary. Today, as then, God agrees to meet with His people in the place where He is worshiped.

"For where two or three gather in my name, there am I with them" (Matt. 18:20).

COMPANION THOUGHT
Do you feel appreciated by your family? Your boss? Do you feel as if God approves of you? Why or why not?

Exodus 40

THE GLORY OF THE LORD

The glory of the Lord filled the tabernacle.
Exodus 40:35

THE TABERNACLE, COVERED WITH BROWN animal skins, appears very plain and ordinary. From the outside, one would never expect to find anything of value. Yet inside, the tabernacle radiates beauty, color, and design. The place of worship, also called the tent of meeting, is an exquisite work of art.

However, what makes the tabernacle unique is not its precious materials and furnishings, but the fact that God dwells there. After the tabernacle is complete, the glory of the Lord fills the sacred space. From that time until the Israelites enter Canaan, God hovers over the sanctuary as a pillar of fire at night, imparting warmth and light. In the daytime, He covers the tabernacle as a cloud, shading the camp from the burning sun. These two visible displays of God's glory lead the Israelites on their journey to the Promised Land. When the pillar and cloud move, God's people move.

The tabernacle is a picture of Christ. Isaiah chapter 53 describes Him as outwardly unadorned and despised by the world (Isa. 53:1–3), but inwardly possessing unspeakable beauty. The glory of God, which once rested over the tabernacle, now dwells within us as His people (the church) and as individual believers. Our hearts become Christ's home (Eph. 3:17; 1 Cor. 6:19–20). As the Holy Spirit guides and protects us on our journey toward our eternal home, God promises, "I will never leave you nor forsake you" (Josh. 1:5).

COMPANION THOUGHT

How do you know when the Holy Spirit is telling you to move on from a particular job, ministry, or relationship? Do you ever feel as if God has "moved on" without you? If so, what could you do about it?

FORTY SIGNIFICANT PEOPLE OF THE BIBLE CHART

Antediluvian Period (Before the Flood) Dates Unknown	Patriarchal Period Dates are best estimates 2200–1800 BC	The Exodus Giving of Law Conquest of Canaan 1525–1375	Period of The Judges 1375–1050	Period of The United Kingdom 1050–930
Bible books covering each period:				
Genesis	Genesis Job	Exodus Leviticus Numbers Deuteronomy Joshua	Judges Ruth 1 Samuel	1 Samuel–2 Samuel 1 Kings 1 Chron–2 Chron Psalms–Proverbs Eccl–S. Songs
Adam	Job	**Moses**	Samson	Saul
Eve	**Abraham**	Aaron	Ruth	**David**
Enoch	Isaac	Joshua	Samuel	Solomon
Noah	Jacob			
	Joseph			

Adam & Eve

Abraham

Canaan →

Joshua

Joseph   Moses

Egypt

Samuel

Saul   David   Solomon

Period of The Divided Kingdom	The Exile And Return	Silence Between Old T New T	Period of The Life of Christ	The Early Church
930–586	586–400	400-5	5 BC–30 AD	30–100 AD
1 Kings-2 Kings 2 Chron Isaiah-Jeremiah Hos-Joel-Amos-Ob Jonah-Micah-Nahum Habakkuk-Zeph	Ezra-Nehemiah Esther Lamentations Ezekiel-Daniel Haggai-Zech Malachi		Matthew Mark Luke John	Acts-Rom-1Cor-2Cor Gal-Eph-Philppns-Col 1Th-2Th-1Tim-2Tim Titus-Phlm-Heb-James 1Peter-2Peter 1Jn-2Jn-3Jn-Jude-Rev
Jeroboam	Ezekiel		Mary	Barnabas
Elijah	Daniel		John/Baptist	**Paul**
Jonah	Esther		**Jesus**	John Mark
Isaiah	Ezra		**Peter**	Luke
Jeremiah	Nehemiah		John	Timothy
			Judas	James

Israel
Judah

Fall of Jerusalem 586 BC

Ezra

Ascension

Babylon

By Floyd E Westbrook

SMALL GROUP GUIDE

THE *BIBLE COMPANION SERIES* ALLOWS members to read and meet at a pace that suits your group. Whether you meet weekly or monthly, the following outline will allow group members to learn from each other's encounters with Scripture. The leader is primarily a facilitator, so it's not necessary for a leader to be a Bible teacher. However, the leader should be familiar with Scripture, willing to direct people to resources when needed, and able to keep the group on track within the agreed upon time schedule.

1. Agree on a meeting schedule: how often, for how long, what day?
2. Agree on a reading pace: not more than six chapters per week is recommended so that the reading load remains manageable.
3. Assign a reading range for each meeting. Encourage members to note:

   - What surprised you?
   - Troubled you?
   - Comforted you?
   - Challenged you?
   - One idea or verse that spoke to you and why.

90-MINUTE STUDY GUIDE

OPENING

15 minutes   Prayer. "Open my eyes that I may see wonderful things in your law" (Ps. 119:18).

Discuss one of the COMPANION THOUGHT questions.

OVERVIEW

10 minutes   OPTION 1: Bible Project Video

If there is access to a computer or video screen, watch a *Bible Project* video relating to the book. Overviews are available for every book of the Bible. (Large books may have more than one). Videos on topics and themes within the books are also available. Each video is approximately seven minutes long. This excellent resource is free at https://bibleproject.com/explore/.

OPTION 2: 5W's and H

Using the classic 5W's and H (Who, What, Where, When, Why, and How), prompt the group to answer these questions based on their reading.

OPTION 3: Leader teaching

Begin with a 2-minute review (what happens in each chapter).

Highlight one or more themes raised in the Bible Companion readings.

STUDY

45 minutes   Learn from each other

Have the group discuss their responses to the assigned passages (see #3).

CLOSING

20 minutes   Blessing

Share concerns. Pray about the concerns and over group members.

Benediction—The Mizpah Prayer

May the Lord keep watch between you and me
when we are away from each other.

Genesis 31:49

NOTES

[1] Tremper Longman III, "Israelite Genres in Their Ancient Near Eastern Context" from *The Changing Face of Form Criticism for the Twenty-First Century* (Grand Rapids, MI: William B. Eerdmans Publishing Company, 2003), 178.

[2] H. Dubrow uses a similar example in her book on genre. *Genre: The Critical Idiom*; (New York: Methuen, 1982), 1–3.

[3] Tremper Longman III, *How to Read the Psalms,* How to Read Series (Downers Grove, IL: InterVarsity Press, 1988), 22.

[4] *NIV Biblical Theology Study Bible*, Genesis 1, Introduction to the Old Testament.

[5] Tremper Longman III and Raymond B Dillard, *An Introduction to the Old Testament* (Grand Rapids, MI; Zondervan, 1994, 2006), 34-35.

[6] *NIV Biblical Theology Study Bible*, Genesis 1, The Pentateuch (T.D. Alexander).

[7] Longman III, Tremper and Scot McKnight, *Genesis, The Story of God Bible Commentary* (Grand Rapids, MI; Zondervan 2016, Kindle Edition), 1.

[8] *Merriam-Webster*, s.v. "genesis," accessed Nov. 9, 2021, http://www.merriam-webster.com/dictionary/genesis.

[9] Tremper Longman III, *How to Read Genesis,* How to Read Series (Downers Grove, IL: InterVarsity Press, 2005), 108–109.

[10] Kenneth Barker, Mark L. Strauss, Jennine K. Brown, Craig L. Bloomberg, and Michael Williams, *The NIV Study Bible, Fully Revised Edition* (Grand Rapids, MI: Zondervan, 2020, e-version), introductory notes.

[11] Jesus as light (John 8:12); as living water (John 4:10–13; Rev. 21:6); as the bread of life (John 6:51); as the vine (John 15:5); and as the source of life (John 11:25).

[12] In the New Testament, Satan is referred to as a serpent: 2 Corinthians 11:3–4; Revelation 12:9 and 20:2.

[13] *NIV Study Bible*, commentary on Genesis 3:15.

[14] The phrase "and then he died" is found eight times in Genesis 5 (vv. 5, 8, 11, 14, 17, 20, 27, 31).

[15] For a deeper look of the role of genealogies in Scripture, see Longman III, Tremper and Scot McKnight, *Genesis, The Story of God Bible Commentary* (Grand Rapids, MI, Zondervan 2016, e-version), 94. Also Longman, *How to Read Genesis*, 121-123.

[16] Longman and McKnight, *Genesis Commentary*, 114.

[17] Longman, *How to Read Genesis*, 114–115.

[18] Longman and McKnight, *Genesis Commentary*, 13, 159.

[19] *Merriam-Webster*, s.v. "covenant," accessed Nov. 9, 2021, http://www.merriam-webster.com/dictionary/covenant.

[20] Five covenants define God's relationship with us and ours with Him: the Noahic, Abrahamic, Mosaic, Davidic, and the New Covenant instituted by Jesus. For further study, see https://bibleproject.com/blog/covenants-the-backbone-bible/.

[21] Longman and McKnight, *Genesis Commentary*, 14.

22 NIV Study Bible, chapter 11:28 notes.

23 NIV Study Bible, chapter 11:31 notes. The moon-god was worshiped both in Ur and Harran.

24 God blessed what Abram had, giving him great wealth (Gen. 13:2; 24:35).

25 Barker, et al., *The NIV Study Bible*, Genesis 12:1.

26 Abraham's interaction with God gives us deeper insight into who God is. God is revealed to be just (Gen. 18:25), righteous (Gen. 18:19), faithful (Gen. 24:27), wise (Gen. 18:25), good (Gen. 19:19), and merciful (Gen. 20:6).

27 Longman, *Read Genesis*, 127.

28 The first covenant was made with Noah. "I establish my covenant with you: Never again will all life be destroyed by the waters of a flood; never again will there be a flood to destroy the earth" (Gen. 9:11).

29 *NIV Study Bible*, Genesis introductory notes.

30 *NIV Study Bible*, Genesis 14:18 notes.

31 Longman, *How to Read Genesis*, 131.

32 Longman and McKnight, *Genesis Commentary*, 220.

33 *NIV Study Bible*, Genesis 19:1 notes.

34 *NIV Study Bible*, Genesis 20:7 notes.

35 *NIV Study Bible*, Genesis 25:26, footnote e. "Heel catcher" is a Hebrew idiom for "deceiver."

36 *NIV Study Bible*, Genesis 32:24 notes.

37 *NIV Study Bible*, Genesis 32:28, footnote f.

38 *NIV Study Bible*, Genesis 31:49, footnote c.

39 *NIV Study Bible*, Genesis 32:24 notes.

40 *NIV Study Bible*, Genesis 32:28, footnote f.

41 "a.nah," "to be humbled," or "to humble oneself," *Step Bible*, Genesis 34:2. For a further explanation, see Longman and McKnight, *Genesis Commentary*, 428.

42 *NIV Cultural Backgrounds Study Bible*, Genesis 34:2 notes, Exodus 22:16–17, and Deuteronomy 22:28–29 (as well as Near Eastern law) had regulations allowing or requiring marriage if a couple has had sexual relations.

43 *NIV Study Bible*, Genesis 40:5 notes.

44 The miraculous birth of Isaac to the aged Abraham and Sarah confirmed God's covenant and was a defining event in Joseph's family history (Gen. 21:1–6).

45 In Genesis 40, Joseph interpreted the dreams of Pharaoh's baker and cupbearer in prison as a favor. Interpreting for Pharaoh is a command performance. Failure could mean death.

46 Jesus wept at Lazarus's tomb (John 11:33–35).

47 Jesus's grief in Gethsemane was so great that He sweat drops of blood (Luke 22:44).

48 In 1 Thessalonians 4:13, Paul makes a distinction between how believers and nonbelievers handle grief. Believers grieve with hope. Jesus's resurrection from the dead proves He is God and is able to restore our lives physically and spiritually.

49 *NIV Study Bible*, Genesis 27:4 and Genesis 27:33 notes.

50 A summary of inheritance rights and birthrights is found in the *NIV Cultural Background Study Bible*, Genesis 25:31 and Genesis 27:4 notes.

51 The tribe of Levi is given no allotment in the Promised Land. The Lord will be their portion (Deut. 18:1–2).

52 *NIV Study Bible*, Genesis 49:1 notes. Also John H. Walton, *Genesis, The NIV Application Commentary* (Zondervan Academic, 2011, e-version), Genesis 49:1–28 notes.

53 John H. Walton, Victor H. Matthews, and Mark W. Chavalas, *The IVP Bible Background Commentary (IVPBBCOT): Old Testament* (Downers Grove, IL: InterVarsity Press, 2000, Kindle Edition), Exodus 1:8–14 notes.

[54] *Merriam-Webster*, s.v. "exodus," accessed Nov. 29, 2021, http://www.merriam-webster.com/dictionary/exodus.

[55] Tremper Longman III, *How to Read Exodus*, How to Read Series (Downers Grove, IL: InterVarsity Press 2009, Kindle Edition), 33.

[56] "Point of View: *Omniscient* means 'all-knowing,' and likewise an omniscient narrator knows every character's thoughts, feelings, and motivations even if that character doesn't reveal any of those things to the other characters." Merriam-webster.com, accessed November 29, 2021, https://www.merriam-webster.com/words-at-play/point-of-view-first-second-third-person-difference.

[57] Longman, *Exodus*, 35.

[58] Kenneth Barker, Mark L. Strauss, Jennine K. Brown, Craig L. Bloomberg, and Michael Williams, *The NIV Study Bible, Fully Revised Edition* (Grand Rapids, MI: Zondervan, 2020, Kindle Edition), Exodus 12:21 notes.

[59] Longman, *Exodus*, 39.

[60] Longman, *Exodus*, 21.

[61] Longman, *Exodus*, 22.

[62] Tremper Longman III and Raymond B Dillard, *An Introduction to the Old Testament* (Grand Rapids, MI: Zondervan, 1994, 2006), 75. See Galatians 2:16. Works do not save us, but obedience proves we love God (1 John 5:2–3).

[63] Tertullian, *The Apology*, trans. S. Thelwall, in *The Ante-Nicene Fathers, Volume III: Latin Christianity: Its Founder, Tertullian* (Buffalo, NY: Christian Literature Company, 1885), 55.

[64] Exodus 2:8–9 tells us Moses's birth mother nursed him and was paid for several years to take care of him. That Aaron comes to visit Moses in the desert of Midian tells us they had a strong bond (Ex. 4:27–28).

[65] Walton, *et al, The IVP Bible Background Commentary*, Exodus 10 notes.

[66] Genesis 37:25–28, 36 and Judges 8:24 identify the Midianites as a subset of the Ishmaelites. Their languages must have been similar as Moses communicated with Jethro and Zipporah (Ex. 2:15–22), but given the distance between the two people groups, the development of a regional dialects would be likely. Mtorah.com notes: "The Moabite language was a Hebrew dialect, and appears on a circa 840 B.C.E. stele about a war between Israel and a Moabite king named Mesha," accessed November 29, 2021, https://mtorah.com/tag/midian/.

[67] "But I have raised you up for this very purpose, that I might show you my power and that my name might be proclaimed in all the earth" (Ex. 9:16).

[68] Deuteronomy 10:16–22 records Moses's call for the people to serve the Lord and only Him.

[69] *NIV Study Bible*, Exodus 2:22 notes.

[70] Abraham (Gen. 17), Moses (Ex. 3), Gideon (Judg. 6–7), Isaiah (Isa. 6), and Paul (Acts 9).

[71] The rod of Aaron becomes a snake in Pharaoh's court (Ex. 7:8–10). God's uses Aaron's rod to turn the Nile to blood (Ex. 7:19–21) and to call the plagues of frogs and gnats down on Egypt (Ex. 8:5–6, 16–17). God uses Moses and his rod to bring down hail (Ex. 9:22), locusts (Ex. 10:12), darkness (Ex. 10:21), to part the Red Sea, and to provide water in the desert (Ex. 17:6; Num. 20:10–13).

[72] Longman, *Exodus*, 35–36.

[73] Biblecharts.org, "The 10 Plagues—Jehovah Versus the God's of Egypt," accessed October 8, 2021, http://biblecharts.org/oldtestament/thetenplagues.pdf.

[74] Longman, *Exodus*, 109–111.

[75] Biblecharts.org, "The 10 Plagues—Jehovah Versus the God's of Egypt," accessed October 8, 2021, http://www.biblecharts.org/oldtestament/thetenlaguesjehovahversusthegodsofegypt.pdf.

76 Charles H. Spurgeon, "The Lesson of the Almond Tree," from a sermon delivered at the Metropolitan Tabernacle, Newington, on April 7, 1881, accessed October 14, 2021, https://www.ccel.org/ccel/spurgeon/sermons46.xxiii.html.

77 In the Old Testament, Abram fled to Egypt during a famine with disastrous results. Abram's lie that Sarai was his sister led to her being taken into a harem (Gen. 12:10–13:2). When God stops Isaac from going to Egypt during another famine, Egypt becomes identified as a place outside of God's promise (Gen. 26:1–2). The metaphor is strengthened when the Hebrews are made slaves in Egypt (Ex. 1:8–11). In the New Testament, Egypt becomes a symbol of slavery and sin (Matthew 2:15; Hebrews 3:16; 8:9; 11:26–27).

78 "The Conversion of Saint Augustine," Early Church History, accessed November 30, 2021, https://earlychurchhistory.org/beliefs-2/the-conversion-of-saint-augustine/.

79 Dan Graves, "John Newton Converted by Amazing Grace," accessed November 30, 2021, https://www.christianity.com/church/church-history/timeline/1701–1800/john-newton-converted-by-amazing-grace-11630250.html.

80 Harvey Whitehouse, "Ritual Modes: Divergent Modes of Ritual, Social Cohesion, Prosociality and Conflict," Centre for the Study of Social Cohesion, accessed December 6, 2021, https://www.cssc.ox.ac.uk/ritual-modes.

81 David Guzik, *Enduring Word Commentary, Jeremiah 15:15–18*, 4.a.i, Thompson, accessed December 8, 2021, https://enduringword.com/bible-commentary/exodus-15.

82 *Merriam-Webster*, s.v. "hymn," accessed December 1, 2021, http://www.merriam-webster.com/dictionary/hymn. In ancient Greece, a hymn praised any deity or hero. Today, a hymn usually refers to a formal poetic song that praises God. Hymns are found throughout the Bible (for example, Hannah's song in I Samuel 2:1–10 in the Old Testament and Philippians 2:6–11 in the New Testament). King David set many of the Psalms to music, establishing hymn poetry as a high form of worship. In Tremper Longman III, *How to Read the Psalms* (Downers Grove, IL: InterVarsity Press, 1988), 46–47.

83 Tremper Longman III, *Confronting Old Testament Controversies: Pressing Questions about Evolution, Sexuality, History, and Violence* (Grand Rapids, MI: Baker, 2019), 176–205.

84 Longman, *How to Read Exodus*, 22.

85 Longman, *Exodus*, 127.

86 "Case law, also used interchangeably with common law, refers to the collection of precedents and authority set by previous judicial decisions on a particular issue or topic." Legal Information Institute, accessed December 1, 2021, https://www.law.cornell.edu/wex/caselaw.

87 Genesis 12:1–3, the Abrahamic covenant.

88 Irving Hexham, *Understanding World Religions: An Interdisciplinary Approach* (Grand Rapids, MI: Zondervan, 2011), Kindle Location (KL) 6479–6480.

89 Justin Taylor, quoting from Tom Schreiner's *40 Questions About Christians and Biblical Law* (Grand Rapids, MI: Kregel Academic, Illustrated edition, 2010), The Gospel Coalition, accessed December 2, 2021, https://www.thegospelcoalition.org/blogs/justin-taylor/what-does-the-word-law-mean-in-the-bible/.

90 Longman and Dillard, *Intro to the Old Testament*, 72. Also, see "The Bible: What Kind of Book Is It?" in the introductory material of this book.

91 *Merriam-Webster*, s.v. "genre," accessed December 2, 2021, http://www.merriam-webster.com/dictionary/genre.

92 Tremper Longman III, *How to Read the Psalms* (Downers Grove, IL: InterVarsity Press, 1988), 22.

[93] The idea of "The Passing and the Permanent" comes from a sermon of Alexander MacLaren by that name. He compares the temporary state of all created things to the permanence of God's kindness and mercy (Isa. 54:10), but applying that same principle to the law helps us discern which laws were given for a specific point in time and which are relevant for all time. *Sermons of Alexander Maclaren*, "The Passing and the Permanent," accessed October 12, 2021, https://biblehub.com/sermons/auth/maclaren/the_passing_and_the_permanent.htm.

[94] Tremper Longman III, *Confronting Old Testament Controversies: Pressing Questions about Evolution, Sexuality, History, and Violence* (Grand Rapids, MI: Baker, 2019), 229–230.

[95] Longman, *OT Controversies*, 230–232.

[96] Longman, *How to Read Exodus*, 63.

[97] Ancient Israel's foreign policy relies on what the New Testament overtly states—that our status as God's children hinges on one thing—faith (Eph. 2:8). If we believe in God, we are family. Later, God will warn against Israelites intermarrying outside the faith (Deut. 7:3), but by the Bible, and registers no disapproval of a person marrying a foreigner who is adopted into the Hebrew clan (see the book of Ruth). Any person who worships Yahweh and identifies with the people of God was to have the same rights as those born as Jews. Caleb, one of the spies who brought back a good report of the Promised Land, was a Kenezite (Num. 32:12). For his service, Caleb receives one of the prized land grants in Canaan (Josh. 14:6–15).

[98] Human beings experience God as a visible divine presence in Numbers 12:8, Isaiah 6:1, and Ezekiel 1:26. However, Jacob, in Genesis 32:22–32, wrestles with God in human form. We can only speculate about what form God took in Exodus 24, but biblical accounts make either manifestation possible.

[99] Longman credits theologian M. G. Kline and biblical scholar K. A. Kitchen with noting the similarities between an ancient Near East treaty and the covenants of the Old Testament. Temper Longman III and Raymond B Dillard, *An Introduction to the Old Testament*, 110–111.

[100] Horns mentioned in Scripture hold different meanings: strength (Deut. 33:17), honor (Lam. 2:3), protection (Dan. 8), triumph (Ps. 89:17; 1 Sam. 2:1), and royalty (Jer. 48:25).

[101] Alexander MacLaren, "The Grasp that Brings Peace," Christian Classics Ethereal Library, accessed December 2, 2021, https://www.ccel.org/ccel/maclaren/isa_jer.ii.i.xxiii.html.

[102] Jesus's last words before ascending into heaven were, "Go into all the world and preach the gospel to all creation" (Mark 16:15).

[103] Chapter 8 of Walter Brueggemann's book *Mandate to Difference* explores these ideas at length, as does his book *Sabbath as Resistance*. Walter Brueggemann, *Sabbath as Resistance: Saying No to the Culture of Now* (Louisville, KY: Westminster John Knox Press, Kindle Edition 2014, 2017), 5, 29, 54, 86, 90.

[104] Clearly, Moses is asking for a revelation of God's presence beyond what has been previously described in Scripture or experienced by Moses and the elders in Exodus 24.

[105] The character of Mesopotamian gods, their limited control in the world, and their motivations are seen in their myths. According to Atrahasis, man was created out of clay and the blood of an evil enemy for the purpose of relieving the gods' workload. Unlike Yahweh, who cares for His creation (Gen. 9:8–17), Mesopotamian gods try to reduce populations by withholding food and water and sending pestilence and disease. Mesopotamian gods can be placated with sacrifices, but gifts do not change the gods' attitudes toward humanity. They are disdainful of us and annoyed by our neediness. Stephanie Dalley, ed. *Myths from Mesopotamia: Creation, the Flood, Gilgamesh, and Others* (Oxford and New York: Oxford University Press, 1989), 4, 20–23.

ORDER INFORMATION

To order additional copies of this book, please visit
www.redemption-press.com.
Also available on Amazon.com and BarnesandNoble.com
or by calling toll-free 1-844-2REDEEM.